English, French, and American Holiday Style

FROM THE EDITORS OF VICTORIA

Copyright ©2025 by Hoffman Media

All rights reserved. No part of this book may be reproduced or transmitted in any form or by any means, electronic or mechanical, including photocopying, or by any information storage and retrieval system, without permission in writing from Hoffman Media. Reviewers may quote brief passages for specific inclusion in a magazine or newspaper.

Hoffman Media
2323 2nd Avenue North
Birmingham, AL 35203
hoffmanmedia.com

ISBN 9798991346955
Printed in China

CONTENTS

9 Introduction

ENGLISH CHARM
10
12 Yuletide Radiance
22 A London Holiday
34 Christmas at Little Latches
44 A Dickensian Celebration
52 Of Novels and Noel
56 In a Manor of Splendor
66 Merriment at the Real Downton Abbey
72 Offering a Boxing Day Tea

JOYEUX NOËL
82
84 From the Château
94 An Escape to Paris
106 Christmas in Provence
116 A Festive Gathering
128 A Fairy-Tale Farmhouse
138 Parfum, Mon Amour
144 A Sideboard of Sweet Temptations

COLONIAL SPLENDOR
152
154 A Return to Simpler Times
164 Observing Christmas in Williamsburg
172 Grand Holiday Estates
188 Branch of History
194 A Cozy Hearthside Repast
202 On the Waterfront in Maine
210 From the Constitution State
215 Memories of Connecticut
216 Wrapped in Colonial Style
218 Warm & Savory

226 Credits & Resources
227 Where to Shop & Buy
228 Recipe Index

INTRODUCTION

At Christmas, favorite destinations seem to shine all the brighter. London and Paris—luminescent in every season but positively gleaming during Yuletide—inspire sojourns to Europe. Along with surveying noted landmarks in these respective cities with esteemed photographers Jane Hope and Georgianna Lane, highlights of our travels abroad include sipping a steaming blend at Fortnum and Mason or sampling macarons at famed pâtisserie Ladurée. Returning to the United States, the most wonderful time of the year draws our hearts to Williamsburg, Virginia. Trimmed with fragrant evergreens and colorful fruits of the season, the historic village reflects the simple joys of centuries past.

With deep appreciation for the places we hold most dear, the editors of *Victoria* magazine present *Splendor of Christmas: English, French, and American Holiday Style*. We begin in England, wandering the magnificent halls of cherished estates and finding repose in a cozy and quaint cottage. Signature fare includes a feast fit for a beloved author and a delectable teatime menu. Continuing to France, we stroll the City of Light, present pastries worthy of the finest salons, and savor a festive Noël. From apartment to château, *brocante* finds bring a certain je ne sais quoi to interiors. Finally, affection for hearth and home beckons us to the United States, where we consider our nation's heritage at estates such as Biltmore and Mount Vernon. Join us in exploring winter in New England, trimming the tree with ornaments from the White House Historical Association, and bringing classic recipes to the table.

Within this volume, discover classic British character, Gallic joie de vivre, and distinctly American sensibilities. Wherever you observe the holidays—on distant shores or within the comfort of home—we hope *Splendor of Christmas* adds radiance to this cherished season.

English CHARM

From Little Aston to London, the beauty of British Yuletide celebrations comes through in elegant décor, treasured heirlooms, and an unparalleled attention to detail. Worthwhile excursions include holiday visits to Castle Howard, Chatsworth, and Highclere Castle. We raise a toast to Charles Dickens with a traditional feast and a tour of his former home. And for the perfect finale, a Boxing Day tea offers sumptuous delights.

YULETIDE RADIANCE

With its Baroque-Palladian architecture, a roofline punctuated by classic statuary, and a majestic dome that rises against the backdrop of Yorkshire's Howardian Hills, Castle Howard is a breathtaking example of England's great country houses— and the perfect setting for a Christmastide gala.

Opposite: A table in the salon is set for the Twelfth Night Dinner, using china, silver, and crystal from the Castle Howard collection. A traditional hanging wreath, made from grape vines procured from the estate's Walled Garden, features characters crafted by designer Gisela Graham.

Upon glimpsing the façade of this impressive manor built for Charles Howard, the 3rd Earl of Carlisle, it is astonishing to think it was designed by a man with nary a bit of design experience. Eschewing notable names in favor of one of his political associates, the earl chose playwright John Vanbrugh to build the home on the site of the ruined Henderskelfe Castle, a property the Howard family acquired through marriage. Vanbrugh wisely enlisted the aid of architect Nicholas Hawksmoor, who brought practical skills to the partnership, and the two created a remarkable and unique residence that has sheltered eight generations of Howard kin.

As the location for several cinematic productions, including the acclaimed mini-series *Brideshead Revisited*, Castle Howard has treated viewers to spectacular scenes of the idyllic grounds, as well as to glimpses of the villa's opulently adorned interiors.

The portrait-lined Grand Staircase leads to the China Landing, where a massive, custom-made cabinet holds more than three hundred pieces of china; the dome of the Great Hall features an ethereal fresco by Venetian artist Giovanni Antonio Pellegrini. Rather than keep this palatial splendor to themselves, the Howard family has graciously chosen to share it, making the estate available for tours and private events.

For more than a decade, Castle Howard has opened its gates and invited the public to share in its grand Yuletide celebration. In 2018, the team of Charlotte Lloyd Webber and Bretta Gerecke orchestrated an extravagant jubilee based on "The Twelve Days of Christmas." The pair brought their mutual backgrounds in theater design to turn a visit to the manor into a magical experience. With help from a brigade of craftspeople and volunteers, the beloved carol came to life. A 25-foot tree was showcased in the Great Hall, where thousands of shimmering fairy lights cascaded over the balcony, while a trio of French hens roosted in Lady Georgiana's dressing room. A traditional Christmas afternoon tea was served in the elegantly appointed Grecian Hall.

The next iteration was just as marvelous, with Charlotte and Bretta presenting "A Christmas Masquerade," inspired by the centuries-old Venetian Carnival. As the name implies, masks were a must. The Long Gallery was transformed into the Grand Canal, and visitors met a comedic cast of characters, engaging in the castle's tradition of pantomime. With each year's theme carried out with similar exuberance, a visit to Castle Howard brings joy to all at this most wonderful time of the year.

Splendor of Christmas | 15

Previous spread: The Castle Howard Bedroom, seen in popular costume drama *Victoria*, is dressed for the holidays, while the Grecian Hall hosts a delightful Christmas Afternoon Tea. Opposite: This dome soars a lofty 70 feet above the Great Hall.

"WHAT WE HAVE TRIED TO DO IS INJECT INTO THE DISPLAY THE THEATRICALITY THAT PLAYWRIGHT JOHN VANBRUGH BROUGHT TO HIS CASTLE HOWARD DESIGN."
—Charlotte Lloyd Webber

Splendor of Christmas | 21

A LONDON HOLIDAY

England's ever-bustling capital becomes increasingly enlivened during December, when the city dresses up for the season. Visitors can expect to find plenty of shopping options—and a seemingly endless variety of tearooms.

Above: Since its founding in 1707, the Fortnum & Mason emporium has been filled to the brim with wonderful offerings. This is especially true during the holiday season. Standing six floors high, Fortnum captivates shoppers with everything from chocolate and Champagne to jewelry and perfume. Right: Five restaurants cater to discriminating taste buds, with afternoon tea served in the Diamond Jubilee Tea Salon. Opposite: On Bond Street, Cartier wraps its façade like a Christmas package, drawing customers in to peruse the brand's iconic watches and jewelry.

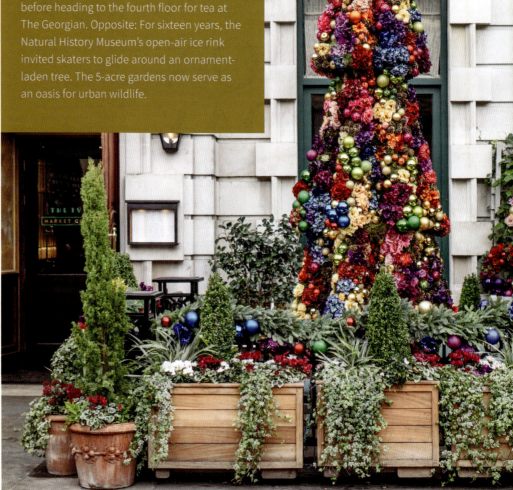

Clockwise from above left: The Lanesborough hotel's elegant setting makes taking tea, complete with freshly baked scones and clotted cream, a true pleasure. Located near the West End theatre district, The Ivy offers diners a chance for celebrity sightings. Lola's Cupcakes bakes their sugary confections fresh every day. Harrods, a long-respected fixture in the Knightsbridge area, is synonymous with luxury. Shoppers may peruse the dazzling range of items before heading to the fourth floor for tea at The Georgian. Opposite: For sixteen years, the Natural History Museum's open-air ice rink invited skaters to glide around an ornament-laden tree. The 5-acre gardens now serve as an oasis for urban wildlife.

Above left: Bea's of Bloomsbury encourages patrons to relax and truly savor every morsel of its brownies, meringues, and more. Twinkling lights lead the way through the Burlington Arcade, opposite, a fifteen-minute drive from the plush Rosewood London, this page, above right. Those with epicurean tastes will appreciate the hotel's special holiday menus, as well as its accessibility to Covent Garden.

Splendor of Christmas | 31

Below right and opposite: Stepping through the revolving doors of The Ritz during the Yuletide season is a breathtaking experience, with an opulently decorated tree soaring upward into the main lobby's dome. A long-standing tradition, tea at The Ritz brings a heightened thrill at Christmastime. This page, above: The Corinthia Hotel London stages a Swan Lake–themed afternoon tea during the holidays.

Splendor of Christmas | 33

CHRISTMAS AT LITTLE LATCHES

Flames crackle and dance in the hearth of a centuries-old home ensconced in England's West Midlands region. In this comfortable abode, the joyous spirit of the season can be found in every endearing nook and cranny.

In the conservatory, an antique French copper pot holds a tree, draped in popcorn-and-cranberry garlands and decorated with wooden stars and tiny faux robins. Sarah Wilton-Basi has collected the cheerful red-and-white linens from various vintage shops.

Above: Rugged wooden beams frame the fireplace in the main lounge, where a vintage hunting horn hangs on the original mantel. Pieces from Sarah's hare-themed collection—a nod to the adorable creatures that bound about the British countryside—appear here and there among vintage books. The tree is strung with fairy lights, illuminating antique glass hearts and straw star ornaments.

As frosty winter winds sweep across the British lowlands, residents from Birmingham to Bromsgrove wrap their scarves a little tighter as they dart in and out of local shops, carrying daunting to-do lists. But in the village of Little Aston in Sutton Coldfield, Sarah Wilton-Basi is happily putting the finishing touches on her holiday décor, warmed by a blazing fire and her enthusiasm for the task at hand.

Sarah and her husband, Param, moved into their circa 1660 semi-detached cottage in 2009 after a six-month renovation restored many of the home's original features. The structure, which formerly served as the local schoolhouse, was christened Little Latches because of the number of latched doors on the property. It is a particularly appropriate venue for Sarah, who taught theatre studies at a performing arts school in Liverpool for many years. Filled with Shakespearean-themed keepsakes, from volumes of plays and poetry to art prints, the shelves are also laden with antique books of classic literature—treasured heirlooms passed down from her great-grandparents.

Param jokes that Sarah starts decorating for Christmas around Easter. She actually waits until mid-December to venture into the garden and surrounding hedgerows to clip fresh greenery, which fills the house with the aromatic fragrance so synonymous with this time of year. She incorporates numerous collections she has curated from craft fairs and her travels abroad, and adds layers of coziness with tartan throws and woolen blankets. Gold-sprayed teasels and fir cones find their way into tabletop vignettes and mantelpiece scenes for an alluring finishing touch.

The lounge is the perfect spot for Yuletide get-togethers. "It is the heart of the cottage," explains Sarah, "and creates a cozy atmosphere in winter." A huge inglenook fireplace spans one wall, and guests naturally converge here to soak up its warmth. The gathering might spill over into the conservatory, where exposed-brick walls lend plenty of character, and expansive windows offer views to the back garden.

When Christmas morning arrives, Sarah will head off for the usual cuddle with her beloved horse, Tilly-Mint, and then celebrate at the barn with friends, both human and equine. Later, she and Param will join family for a special dinner with all the trimmings before making their way home to enjoy a bit of mulled wine before the fire in the blissful comfort of Little Latches.

"CHRISTMAS IN ENGLAND IS ESSENTIALLY ABOUT BEING AROUND FAMILY AND FRIENDS, SHARING IN ALL THAT IS GOOD." —Sarah Wilton-Basi

Brimming from a basket, silvery birch logs serve as fuel for the fire in the conservatory's wood-burning stove. Atop the mantel, a pretty mix of fir, holly, dried hydrangeas, and fir cones forms a festive garland.

Above left: A stained glass window that opens like a porthole adds a bit of character to the conservatory. Above right: Mince pies are traditional English Christmas fare. Opposite: Lit by candles of varying heights, a scattering of greenery, berries, and dried blooms lends seasonal charm to an inglenook fireplace.

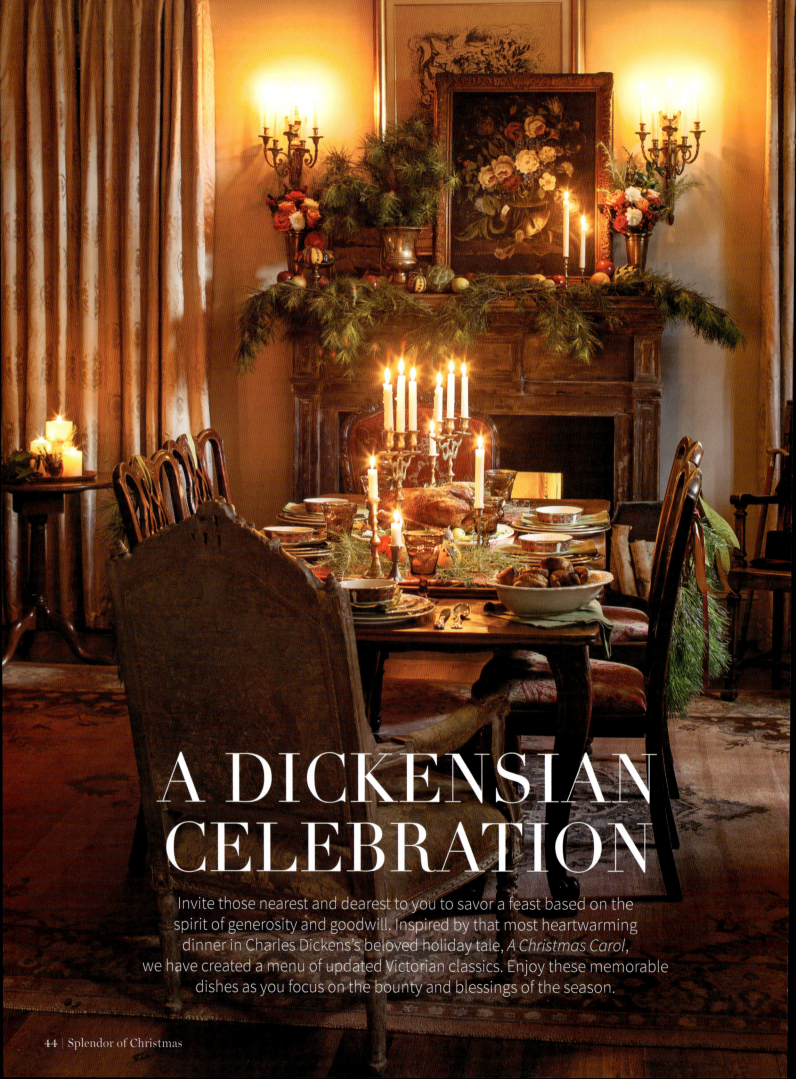

A DICKENSIAN CELEBRATION

Invite those nearest and dearest to you to savor a feast based on the spirit of generosity and goodwill. Inspired by that most heartwarming dinner in Charles Dickens's beloved holiday tale, *A Christmas Carol*, we have created a menu of updated Victorian classics. Enjoy these memorable dishes as you focus on the bounty and blessings of the season.

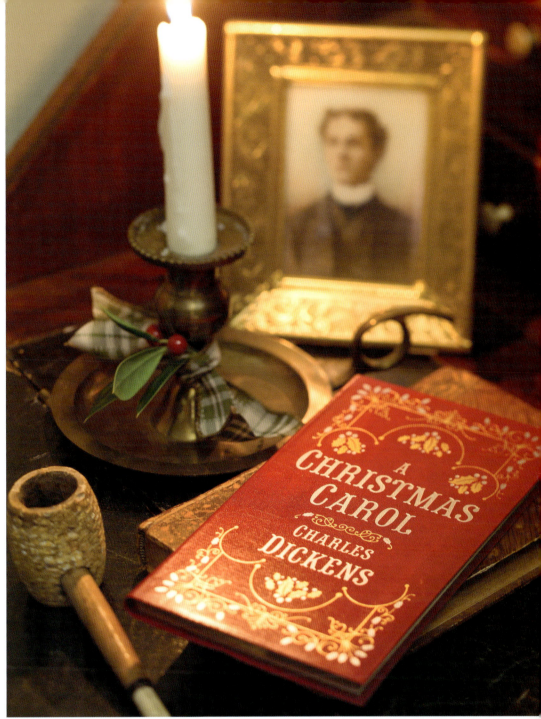

Opposite: Fragrant fir boughs, winter fruit, a bevy of blooms, and candlelight create a homelike ambience for an elegant repast that will not soon be forgotten. This page, clockwise from below right: Serve glasses of festive Smoking Bishop—a spiced-wine punch garnished with citrus slices, cinnamon sticks, and nutmeg—to set the tone for an evening of celebration. Placed on a nearby desk, beautifully penned words from Charles Dickens convey the change of heart that Christmas can bring. For a perfect first course, rich Oyster Soup is ladled steaming from a tureen. Adding to the scene, a rare copy of the classic book is certain to captivate guests.

"FOR IT IS GOOD TO BE CHILDREN SOMETIMES, AND NEVER BETTER THAN AT CHRISTMAS, WHEN ITS MIGHTY FOUNDER WAS A CHILD HIMSELF."

—Charles Dickens

Opposite: A tartan-covered table is set with festive holiday china and pressed cranberry glass goblets. Decorated by hand with care, plump oranges studded with spicy cloves are tucked into greenery for a charming centerpiece. This page, above: In the fictional tale, Tiny Tim Cratchit blessed the Christmas goose, proclaiming, "God bless us, every one!" Our magnificent interpretation is roasted with herbs and aromatic vegetables and encircled by crab apples, figs, and sage. Right: Airy Yorkshire Puddings, prepared using rich pan drippings, rise to great heights as they are baked. The side dish is flavored with rosemary, parsley, and black pepper.

Clockwise from above left: Honor the Christmas spirit with a tableau of fresh flowers and fruit. Nutty brown butter combined with sage and garlic flavor sour creamy Mashed Potatoes. Victorian edible delights include nuts in the shell, which are pleasing to both the eye and the palate. Encourage your guests to wear old-fashioned holiday attire to the gathering. Roasting enhances the color and taste of winter's favorite root vegetables; parsnips, radishes, carrots, turnips, and beets glimmer like a bowl full of ornaments.

This page: Jovial wishes for a happy Christmas ring out as Figgy Pudding is served. The spiced dessert, infused with dried fruit and gently steamed in a vintage mould, is placed on a platter, drizzled with Cinnamon-Caramel Sauce, and bejeweled with figs.

RECIPE INDEX

Smoking Bishop
Makes 6 to 8 servings

4 **navel oranges**
4 tablespoons whole **cloves**
2 **lemons**
1 (750-mL) bottle **Beaujolais**
3 pieces **candied ginger**
4 **cardamom pods**
3 **allspice berries**
2 **star anise pods**
¾ cup firmly packed **light brown sugar**
3 **cinnamon sticks**
1 (750-mL) bottle **port**
Garnish: **orange slices, lemon slices, cinnamon sticks,** and freshly grated **nutmeg**

1. Preheat oven to 300°. Line a rimmed baking sheet with aluminum foil; set aside.
2. Stud oranges with cloves. Place oranges and lemons on prepared pan. Bake until lightly browned, 45 minutes to 1 hour.
3. Remove from oven and place in a large bowl. Add Beaujolais, ginger, cardamom, allspice, star anise, and brown sugar, whisking to combine. Cover tightly and let sit at room temperature for 24 hours.
4. Remove oranges and lemons from mixture. Cut fruit and squeeze juice into wine mixture; discard fruit.
5. Transfer wine mixture to a saucepan; add cinnamon sticks. Cook over medium-high heat for 5 minutes. Reduce heat to low and add port; gently simmer for 15 minutes. Increase heat to high and heat just until smoking hot, about 2 minutes. Remove from heat. Garnish each serving with an orange slice, a lemon slice, a cinnamon stick, and a pinch of nutmeg, if desired.

Oyster Soup
Makes 6 to 8 servings

3 slices **bacon**, diced
⅓ cup **vegetable oil**
⅓ cup **all-purpose flour**
2 cups chopped **yellow onion**
1 cup chopped **leeks**
1 cup chopped **green onion**
2 tablespoons minced **garlic**
6 cups warm **milk** (110°–120°)
4 (8-ounce) cans **oysters**, liquor drained and reserved, or 48 freshly shucked **oysters**, liquor reserved
6 tablespoons **butter**
¼ cup chopped fresh **parsley**
1 tablespoon **kosher salt**
2 teaspoons ground **black pepper**
1½ cups **heavy whipping cream**
Garnish: chopped **green onion** and **celery leaves**

1. In a large Dutch oven, cook bacon over medium-high heat until crisp. Remove bacon and let drain on paper towels, reserving 1 tablespoon drippings in pan. Add oil to drippings over medium-high heat. Add flour and cook, stirring constantly, until a light brown roux forms, 2 to 3 minutes. Add yellow onion, leeks, green onion, and garlic. Cook, stirring often, until tender, about 5 minutes.
2. Meanwhile, in a large bowl, combine milk and reserved oyster liquor.
3. Reduce heat to medium. Gradually add milk mixture to onion mixture, stirring constantly. Mixture will thicken slightly. Bring mixture to a low boil. Reduce heat to medium-low; simmer for 2 minutes.
4. Add oysters, butter, parsley, salt, and pepper. Simmer until oyster edges begin to curl, about 3 to 5 minutes. Stir in cream, whisking to combine. Remove from heat. Garnish with crumbled reserved bacon, green onion, and celery leaves, if desired.

Roasted Christmas Goose
Makes 6 to 8 servings

1 (12- to 14-pound) dressed frozen **goose**, thawed
3 tablespoons **kosher salt**, divided
1½ tablespoons ground **black pepper**, divided
4 stalks **celery**, chopped
4 **carrots**, chopped
2 **yellow onions**, chopped
4 sprigs fresh **thyme**
4 sprigs fresh **sage**
2 cups **chicken broth**
Garnish: **crab apples, figs, celery leaves,** and fresh **sage**

1. With rack set at lowest level, preheat oven to 400°. Place a wire rack in a large roasting pan; set aside.
2. With paper towels, pat goose dry inside and out. Using a sharp knife, trim excess fat from cavity; reserve. If necessary, remove first and second joints of wings; reserve, if desired. Carefully prick skin of goose, making sure flesh stays intact. Fold neck flap under goose and secure with toothpicks.
3. Sprinkle cavity with 2 tablespoons salt and 1 tablespoon pepper. Stuff with half of celery, carrots, and onions. Insert thyme and sage into cavity. To prepared pan, add remaining half of celery, carrots, and onions; broth; and reserved fat. Place goose, breast side up, on prepared rack. Season with remaining 1 tablespoon salt and remaining ½ tablespoon pepper.
4. Roast goose for 45 minutes, basting with pan drippings every 20 minutes. Reduce oven temperature to 300°. Continue roasting until a meat thermometer registers 180° when inserted into breast, away from bone, and goose is golden brown, about 1½ hours. Remove goose from oven, and let rest for 15 to 20 minutes. Transfer to a serving platter, reserving pan drippings. Garnish with crab apples, figs, celery leaves, and sage, if desired.

Yorkshire Puddings
Makes 12 servings

4 tablespoons **pan drippings**, reserved from Roasted Christmas Goose
1½ cups **all-purpose flour**
1 tablespoon **dried parsley flakes**
1 tablespoon chopped fresh **rosemary**
2 large **eggs**
1 **egg white**
1¾ cups **whole milk**
2 teaspoons **kosher salt**
½ teaspoon freshly ground **black pepper**

1. Preheat oven to 425°.
2. In each well of a 12-well muffin pan, place 1 teaspoon reserved drippings. Place pan in oven to heat and remove when drippings begin to smoke.
3. In a small bowl, combine flour, parsley, rosemary, eggs, egg white, milk, salt, and pepper, whisking until smooth. Divide batter among prepared wells, filling each approximately two-thirds full. Immediately place in

oven, and bake for 20 to 25 minutes, or until puffed, crisp, and browned. Let cool in pan on a wire rack for 5 minutes before serving.

Sage and Browned Butter Mashed Potatoes
Serves 6 to 8

8 cups **water**
3 **russet potatoes**, peeled and chopped
¼ cup plus 1½ teaspoons **kosher salt**, divided
1 cup **butter**
6 fresh **sage leaves**
2 tablespoons **vegetable oil**
3 cloves **garlic**, minced
1 (3-ounce) package **cream cheese**, softened
1 teaspoon ground **black pepper**
½ cup **half-and-half**

1. In a large pot over high heat, bring 8 cups water to a boil. Add potatoes and ¼ cup salt and simmer over medium-high heat until tender, 5 to 8 minutes.
2. In a medium saucepan, melt butter over medium-high heat. Add sage and cook until leaves are crisp and butter turns a medium-brown color. Remove from heat and transfer to a bowl.
3. Over medium-high heat, add oil to pan. Add garlic and cook until browned. Remove from heat and set aside.
4. Drain potatoes and return to pot. Add ½ cup browned butter, reserving sage leaves. Add garlic, cream cheese, pepper, half-and-half, and remaining 1½ teaspoons salt; mash until creamy. Top with remaining ½ cup browned butter and sage leaves. Serve immediately.

Roasted Root Vegetables
Serves 6

1 (16-ounce) bag **parsnips**, peeled, trimmed, and chopped
1 bunch **radishes**, trimmed and halved, with green tops intact
1 bunch **carrots**, peeled and trimmed, with green tops intact
4 **turnips**, peeled and quartered
4 **shallots**, peeled and quartered
3 **yellow beets**, peeled and quartered
4 cloves **garlic**, peeled
⅓ cup **olive oil**
1 tablespoon **kosher salt**
2 teaspoons freshly **ground black pepper**
Garnish: fresh **thyme**

1. Preheat oven to 425°.
2. On a large baking sheet lined with foil, place parsnips, radishes, carrots, turnips, shallots, beets, and garlic. Pour olive oil over vegetables and toss to coat. Sprinkle with salt and pepper. Bake until fork tender, 15 to 20 minutes. Garnish with thyme, if desired. Serve immediately.

Figgy Pudding
Makes 6 servings

1 cup diced **dried Calimyrna figs**
1 cup diced **dried apricots**
½ cup **golden raisins**
¾ cup **water**
2 teaspoons **vanilla extract**
1 cup **spiced rum**, divided
½ cup **dried cherries**
1½ cups **all-purpose flour**
2 teaspoons **baking powder**
1 teaspoon ground **cinnamon**
½ teaspoon ground **ginger**
¼ teaspoon ground **cardamom**
¼ teaspoon **salt**
3 large **eggs**
1 cup firmly packed **light brown sugar**
½ cup **unsalted butter**, melted
1½ cups **bread crumbs**
½ cup **fig preserves**
2¼ cups **Cinnamon-Caramel Sauce** (recipe follows)
Garnish: **figs**

1. Preheat oven to 350°. Spray a 4-cup stainless steel mould with baking spray. Place mould in a roasting pan.
2. In a saucepan, combine figs, apricots, raisins, and ¾ cup water over medium-high heat. Bring to a boil; reduce heat and simmer until water has almost evaporated, about 3 minutes. Add vanilla extract and ⅔ cup rum; simmer until mixture is reduced to ¼ cup, 5 to 10 minutes.
3. In a small bowl, combine remaining ⅓ cup rum and cherries. Let mixture macerate for at least 20 minutes.
4. In a medium bowl, combine flour, baking powder, cinnamon, ginger, cardamom, and salt.
5. In a separate medium bowl, whisk together eggs, brown sugar, and melted butter. Add fruit mixture and stir to combine. Add egg mixture to flour mixture, stirring just until combined. Fold in cherries, bread crumbs, and fig preserves.
6. Pour batter into prepared mould, filling to 1 inch from top. Carefully pour boiling-hot water into base of roasting pan until water level reaches halfway up mould. Cover mould tightly with foil and place roasting pan in oven. Bake until pudding is set, 1 to 1½ hours.
7. Remove pan from oven and let water cool completely. Remove mould from water bath. Run a knife around edge of mould to loosen pudding. Place a serving dish on top of mould, and invert pudding onto dish. Serve warm with Cinnamon-Caramel Sauce. Garnish with figs, if desired.

Cinnamon-Caramel Sauce
Makes approximately 2¼ cups

1½ cups **water**
3 **cinnamon sticks**
2 cups **granulated sugar**
4 tablespoons **butter**
¾ cup **heavy whipping cream**
2 tablespoons **spiced rum**

1. In a medium saucepan, bring 1½ cups water and cinnamon sticks to a boil over medium-high heat. Reduce heat to medium and simmer for 5 minutes. Remove from heat and steep for 15 minutes. Remove cinnamon sticks.
2. Return pan to stove. Add sugar and cook over medium-high heat, stirring occasionally, until mixture reaches 340° on a candy thermometer. Remove from heat. Add butter, whisking until melted. Add cream and whisk until smooth. Add rum and whisk until combined. Let mixture cool completely. Store at room temperature in an airtight container for up to 3 days.

OF NOVELS AND NOEL

A quaint stroll down London's Doughty Street leads to an unassuming terraced Georgian abode-turned-museum that offers a glimpse into the literary history of the author credited with popularizing beloved Christmas traditions and penning international classics.

In 1837, years before titles such as *Great Expectations* and *David Copperfield* were written, Charles Dickens, his wife Catherine, and their ever-growing family settled into a modest brick residence in the Bloomsbury district of London's West End.

Within these walls, the burgeoning author completed installments of *The Pickwick Papers*, the syndicated series that gave voice to Britain's working class and helped launch his lifelong career as a writer, and began drafting another recognizable work, *Oliver Twist*.

When the Dickens family's lease ended, the building was used as a boarding house for several decades until the Dickens Fellowship, an international association dedicated to the life and works of the novelist, purchased the property in 1923, opening the residence to the public as a museum in 1925. Crossing the threshold today, visitors encounter life as it was in Victorian-era London, with rooms decorated in traditional furnishings and curated displays of Dickens's own belongings.

Tour guides dressed in period attire lead guests through the museum's five floors, with stops in the formal dining room, nursery, and an outdoor courtyard oasis where one can enjoy refreshments onsite at The Pickwick Café. In celebration of Dickens's most popular novella, *A Christmas Carol*, the museum decks the halls for wintertime; live reenactments of the beloved tale can be enjoyed among twinkling Christmas trees and festive treats. Visitors who experience this charming exhibition concur Dickens's message: "I am light as a feather, I am as happy as an angel … . A merry Christmas to everybody!"

Splendor of Christmas | 55

IN A MANOR OF SPLENDOR

Dressed in an exuberant array of lights, garland, and imaginative displays bursting with storybook appeal, England's "Palace of the Peak" issues an invitation for one and all to step into a realm of unparalleled enchantment.

Above: Offering a stately welcome, the Painted Hall is the largest and most impressive space in the original house. Taking its cues from the room's magnificent works of art, the Christmas tree is trimmed with a shimmering assortment of amber and blue ornaments. Opposite: In the library, long strands of ribbon hold holiday cards filled with happy sentiments. Behind them, neatly ordered on the shelves, rests part of Chatsworth's 40,000-volume book collection.

No matter the season, a feeling of elation stirs the heart as the spectacular façade of Chatsworth emerges amidst the rolling hills of Derbyshire. Poised on the banks of the River Derwent, its gilded window frames glinting in the sun, the palatial house and grounds seem spun from the thread of legends. In fact, the estate has been home to seventeen generations of the Devonshire family for nearly five centuries—long serving as the setting for elaborate fêtes quite literally fit for a queen. Within the sumptuous interiors, silver candelabras parade down the dining table, while frescoed ceilings soar above marble floors and collections of art, sculpture, and books considered among the most significant in Britain. But Christmas sprinkles these treasures and storied halls with an extra layer of grandeur.

Drawing inspiration from history and literature, each year a new theme gives flight to fresh Yuletide fancies. Stories spring to life, summoning up scenes from Narnia or the delicate spokes of Cinderella's carriage. Guides dressed in Dickensian attire appear alongside Victorian shop fronts and actors portraying Scrooge or Miss Havisham. The Mad Hatter partakes of tea with Alice. Surprises abound around each corner as the house is cleverly transformed into a captivating wonderland lit by the ethereal glow of thousands of fairy lights and a multitude of towering Christmas trees glittering with baubles and bulbs. Visitors from far and wide pass through the heavy oak doors, entranced by the spectacle.

Outdoors, the holiday spirit is shaken and poured out in equal measure across the vast gardens and farmyards. Muffled against midwinter's crisp air, guests wander illuminated pathways where cheerful melodies fill the air, and light shows animate the home's exterior. A Christmas market crowns the festive outing, offering stalls brimming with special trinkets, crafts, and ornaments—small tokens to remember a grand celebration.

Opposite: Garlanded with a multitude of twinkling lights and hundreds of decorative flourishes, the chapel's evergreen immediately draws the eye upward to a majestic altarpiece and lofty ceilings. Painted by Louis Laguerre around 1690, the ceiling depicts Christ in Glory, on his ascension into heaven. Constructed of alabaster and black marble, the altarpiece is a triumph of design by Chatsworth's master carver Samuel Watson. Oil painting *The Incredulity of St. Thomas* by Antonio Verrio crowns the structure and is flanked by the standing figures of Justice and Faith, carved by Caius Gabriel Cibber.

Splendor of Christmas | 61

Bringing Christmas to life at Chatsworth is a continuous endeavor. Themes are determined at least two years in advance to allow adequate time for planning and construction. Many of the decorations and installations are hand-crafted by staff who work closely with artists and makers on special commissions or bespoke artwork for some displays. Production often begins in summer as baubles are wired, Christmas stockings are sewn, and other fanciful embellishments are made to grace the rooms. Two weeks before the house opens its doors for the holiday season, decorating begins in earnest. Both real and artificial trees are brought in by the house and landscape team, and a dedicated brigade of talented individuals begins the magical transformation.

Splendor of Christmas | 63

From its inception, Chatsworth was designed to entertain, and the holidays have always been a busy period filled with family visitors and guests. During the 1920s and 1930s, records show that there were often up to 150 people in the house for the Yuletide season. Christmas morning was spent attending church and opening some presents. Luncheon, featuring traditional English dishes such as plum pudding and mince pies, would be followed by substantial outdoor exercise and afternoon tea with Christmas cake. Then the tree would be lit in the Painted Hall, and the Duke and Duchess would give out their packages, including gifts for the entire household and visiting servants. Today, thousands of guests pass through the doors each day from November to early January, seeking delight in the estate's Christmas festivities. Admission during this peak season operates on a timed basis, so prebooking tickets is essential.

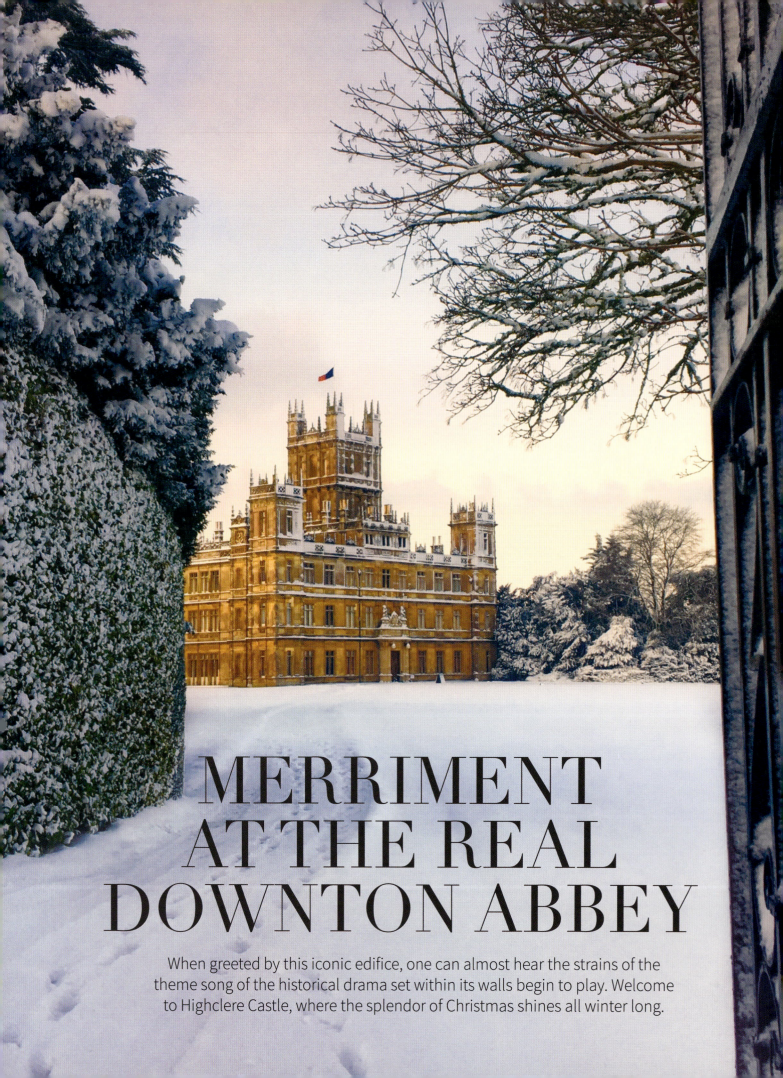

MERRIMENT AT THE REAL DOWNTON ABBEY

When greeted by this iconic edifice, one can almost hear the strains of the theme song of the historical drama set within its walls begin to play. Welcome to Highclere Castle, where the splendor of Christmas shines all winter long.

Splendor of Christmas | 67

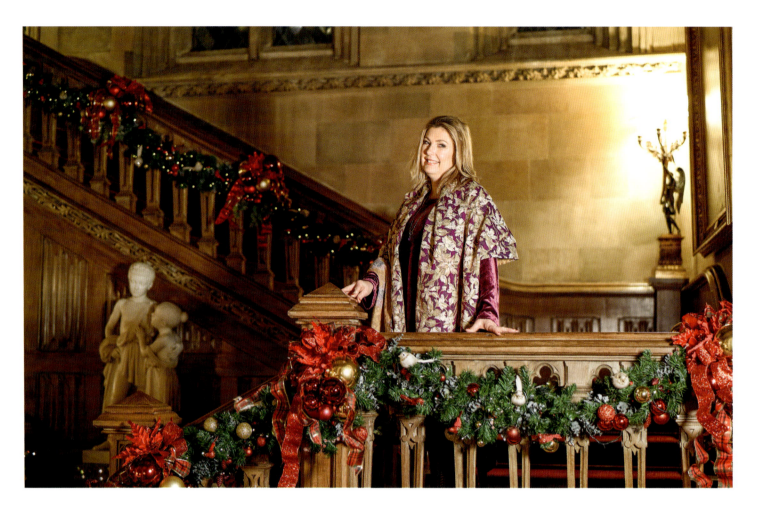

Above: *Victoria*'s esteemed 2025 Lady-in-Residence The Countess of Carnarvon stands behind the festooned balustrade of the Oak Staircase, which leads from the Saloon at the heart of the castle. Opposite: Vaulted ceilings and a gallery view of the upper floor give way to the welcoming sight of Highclere Castle's massive Christmas tree. The fairy figure that crowns this evergreen is the first decoration to be attached before the spruce is carefully erected.

From Advent to Boxing Day and even beyond, the whole of December brings jubilee to Highclere Castle. The Countess of Carnarvon describes the Grade I listed country house in Hampshire, England, as "above all a Victorian home, the period in which the Christmas we know and love today was developed."

On the first of the month, a twenty-foot, locally grown Norway spruce makes its appearance in the Saloon, a grand room situated at the heart of the home. This task is, of course, a massive undertaking that requires the help of devoted staff members, who transport the colossal evergreen through the castle and adorn it in splendid lights and baubles. Other trees throughout the estate are joined by garlands, poinsettias, and handmade wreaths that deck the halls in merriment.

In the following weeks, Highclere is open to invited guests for various midwinter entertaining, especially in the form of cocktail and dinner parties, typically with philanthropic undertones (each year the Earl and Countess choose a different charity to support). In the green silk-walled Drawing Room, the family's heirloom Steinway piano has welcomed many talented guests to tickle the ivories over the years, including John Lunn, who wrote the music for *Downton Abbey*. At Christmas, the instrument is home to dozens of cards that have made their way to the castle by post—proudly displaying the visages of beloved friends and family and their holiday greetings.

On the 23rd of December, guest rooms are prepared in the castle, awaiting the presence of close family members who come to stay for Christmas. By that evening, they—and, hopefully, a sprinkling of alabaster snowflakes—have safely arrived. On Christmas Eve, as the sun makes its descent and children's thoughts can't help but turn to Santa Claus's impending appearance, the Earl gathers the young ones in the Library. Settled in a red armchair beside a crackling fire, he reads aloud: "'Twas the night before Christmas, when all through the house … ." As lights are put out and everyone is tucked into bed, the Saloon fireplace is reserved for Father Christmas, with a glass of brandy, plate of mince pies, and bundle of leafy carrots left for him and his reindeer to enjoy.

On Christmas morn, the Countess and her Labradors take their usual stroll about the grounds, their ears greeted first by the delightful chatter of children discovering tokens left at the foot of their beds in the night. The family then attends worship at their circa 1870 church, St Michael and All Angels, before gathering 'round the table for a feast starring a roast turkey and the long-awaited Christmas pudding. In past years, the afternoon would wind down with a gathering in Lady Carnarvon's study to watch Queen Elizabeth II's annual Christmas message. Finally, when new episodes were being aired, the party would indulge in what the Countess calls "the greatest fun": viewing the special Christmas episode of *Downton Abbey*, filmed, of course, within the walls of Highclere Castle.

Splendor of Christmas | 71

OFFERING A BOXING DAY TEA

Observed in the British Commonwealth on the day after Christmas, Boxing Day is marked by the bestowing of gifts to service workers. Carry on this generous spirit by encouraging guests of a festive teatime gathering to bring donations for those in need.

Opposite: Boughs of holly lend quintessential English charm to interiors. Cut stems hold their color for weeks, adding beauty that lasts well into winter. This page: Ribbons of citrus glaze offer the final grace note to Orange-Scented Pear Turnovers, delectable packages of fruit filling wrapped in flaky puff pastry.

Opposite: Studded with flecks of orange zest, dried tropical fruit, and toasted coconut, our recipe for Ambrosia Scones brings flavors of the classic dessert to the tea menu. This page: Touches of red and green draw the eye to Prosciutto, Tomato, and Ricotta Tarts. At home on a pedestaled server for teatime, this savory dish pairs equally well with salad for a refreshing winter lunch.

"MISTLETOE AND GLEAMING HOLLY, SYMBOLS OF A BLESSED DAY."
—Louisa May Alcott

RECIPE INDEX

Orange-Scented Pear Turnovers
Makes 32

6 **pears**, peeled, cored, and diced
1½ cups **Chardonnay**
1 cup **granulated sugar**
½ cup **pear preserves**
1 tablespoon **orange zest**
½ teaspoon ground **cardamom**
1 (17.3-ounce) package frozen **puff pastry**, thawed
1½ cups **confectioners' sugar**
3 tablespoons fresh **orange juice**
1 teaspoon **orange extract**

1. Preheat oven to 400°. Line a baking sheet with parchment paper.
2. In a medium saucepan, combine pears, Chardonnay, granulated sugar, pear preserves, orange zest, and cardamom over medium heat; stir until well combined. Cook until reduced by a third, about 15 minutes. Remove from heat; let cool completely.
3. On a lightly floured surface, unfold pastry sheets and lightly dust with flour. Roll each sheet into a 12x12-inch square. Cut dough into 3x3-inch squares. Place equal amounts filling (approximately 1 teaspoon) on center of each square.
4. Dip a fingertip in water and moisten edges of each square. Fold dough over to form triangles, gently pressing to remove air pockets around filling. Press edges of dough together and use a fork to crimp and seal edges of each turnover. Arrange on prepared pan.
5. Bake until golden brown, 15 to 18 minutes. Transfer to wire racks to let cool slightly.
6. In a small bowl, combine confectioners' sugar, orange juice, and orange extract. Drizzle turnovers with glaze and serve warm.

Note: Turnovers may be filled and shaped up to 2 hours before baking. Cover tightly with plastic wrap and refrigerate.

Ambrosia Scones
Makes 12

2½ cups **all-purpose flour**
½ cup plus 2 tablespoons **granulated sugar**, divided
2 teaspoons **baking powder**
½ teaspoon **salt**
½ cup **unsalted butter**, cubed
1 (3-ounce) package **cream cheese**, cubed
1 (16-ounce) package **dried tropical fruit**, chopped
1 tablespoon **orange zest**
½ cup **toasted coconut**
⅓ cup **heavy whipping cream**
1 teaspoon **coconut extract**

1. Preheat oven to 375°. Line 2 baking sheets with parchment paper.
2. In a large bowl, combine flour, ½ cup sugar, baking powder, and salt. Using a pastry blender or 2 forks, cut in butter and cream cheese until mixture is crumbly. Add dried fruit, orange zest, and coconut; stir to combine.
3. In a small bowl, combine cream and coconut extract. Add cream mixture to flour mixture, stirring just until dry ingredients are moistened.
4. On a lightly floured surface, roll dough to ¾-inch thickness. Using a 3-inch biscuit cutter, cut scones. Place on prepared pans, and sprinkle with remaining 2 tablespoons sugar.
5. Bake until light golden brown, 13 to 15 minutes.

Prosciutto, Tomato, and Ricotta Tarts
Makes 12 (4-inch) tarts

1 (14.1-ounce) package **refrigerated piecrusts**
2 (8-ounce) containers **ricotta cheese**
4 large **eggs**, lightly beaten
1 (4-ounce) package **prosciutto**, diced
¼ cup loosely packed chopped fresh **basil**
¼ cup loosely packed chopped fresh **oregano**
½ teaspoon **salt**
½ teaspoon ground **black pepper**
1½ cups **Parmesan cheese**
1 pint **cherry tomatoes**, sliced into thin rounds
Garnish: fresh **basil**

1. Preheat oven to 450°. Lightly spray 12 (4-inch) tart pans with cooking spray.
2. On a lightly floured surface, roll piecrusts to ⅛-inch thickness. Using a 4½-inch round cutter, cut 12 circles from dough. Evenly press rounds into bottoms and up sides of prepared pans; prick bottoms with a fork. Place on a baking sheet.
3. Bake until golden brown, 7 to 8 minutes. Let cool on wire racks for 5 minutes; remove tart shells from pans and let cool completely.
4. In a large bowl, whisk together ricotta and eggs until smooth. Add prosciutto, basil, oregano, salt, and pepper.
5. Reduce oven temperature to 350°. Line 2 baking sheets with parchment paper.
6. Place crusts on prepared pans. Evenly spoon ricotta mixture into each crust. Evenly sprinkle each tart with Parmesan, and place 3 to 4 tomato slices on top. Using fingertips, gently press tomatoes into filling.
7. Bake until golden brown, about 25 minutes. Let cool on pans for 5 minutes; transfer to wire racks to let cool completely. Garnish with basil, if desired. Serve at room temperature.

Note: Tarts can be made ahead and refrigerated in an airtight container for up to 2 days. Reheat before serving.

Chicken Salad Sandwiches with Cranberry-Apricot Chutney
Makes 18 tea sandwiches

1 **rotisserie chicken**, meat coarsely chopped
1 (3-ounce) package **cream cheese**, softened
¼ cup **mayonnaise**
1 tablespoon chopped **green onion**
1 teaspoon chopped fresh **sage**
1 teaspoon chopped fresh **thyme**

¼ teaspoon **salt**
¼ teaspoon ground **black pepper**
⅛ teaspoon **celery salt**
1 loaf thinly sliced **white bread**
½ cup chopped **toasted pecans**
Cranberry-Apricot Chutney (recipe follows)
Garnish: fresh **parsley**

1. In a medium bowl, combine chicken, cream cheese, and mayonnaise. Stir to combine. Add green onion, sage, thyme, salt, pepper, and celery salt.
2. Cut crusts off of bread. Evenly spread a thin layer of chicken salad on 1 bread slice and top with a second slice. Repeat with remaining chicken salad and bread. Cut each sandwich in half diagonally.
3. Place toasted pecans in a shallow bowl. Gently press edges of each sandwich into pecans to coat. Place approximately 1 teaspoon Cranberry-Apricot Chutney on top of each sandwich. Garnish with parsley, if desired.

Cranberry-Apricot Chutney
Makes approximately 2 cups

1 (8-ounce) package fresh **cranberries**
1 (7-ounce) package **dried apricots**, chopped
⅔ cup **apricot preserves**
½ cup **water**
1 **shallot**, finely diced

1. In a medium saucepan, combine cranberries, apricots, preserves, ½ cup water, and shallot over medium heat; cook until reduced by a third, about 20 minutes.
2. Remove from heat and let cool completely. Refrigerate until ready to use.

Joyeux NOËL

Escape to the countryside, where a centuries-old château brims with European finds, a chic Provençal abode boasts romantic style, and a welcoming farmhouse shelters brocante *finds. Stroll the avenues of the City of Light in search of radiant treasures— taking inspiration from Paris's storied salons to plan convivial gatherings that greet the season with the sweet sophistication and irresistible allure of France.*

FROM THE CHÂTEAU

Carefully curated antiques, hand-crafted wares, and other finds lend seasonal charm to a storied home in Sézanne, France.

Splendor of Christmas | 85

In the village of Sézanne, in the Champagne region of France, Pascale and Olivier Gisclard happened upon a property for purchase that had once belonged to a cousin of Empress Joséphine de Beauharnais, who likely visited the home. The house was built in the 1700s and remodeled in the nineteenth century, but in recent years it had fallen into a state of disrepair. Pascale and Olivier saw beyond the dust and cobwebs and visualized it as the perfect location for their professional endeavors.

The ground floor features double doors throughout, and the enclosed garden and courtyard not only add beauty and charm, but also provide an ideal spot for displaying outdoor antiques. As the owners set about gently restoring the house, they discovered, to their delight, original wood paneling and painting from the Louis XV period in their favorite rooms: a series of four linked living areas, including one dubbed the Salon de la Marquise.

Intrepid collectors Pascale and Olivier have been involved in interior design for decades, traveling extensively to amass an expansive trove of wares from England, Italy, Sweden, and France. For many years, they filled their historic French château with extraordinary finds and opened it to the public twice annually for a memorable sale known as Le Grillon Voyageur (which charmingly translates to The Traveling Cricket).

Pascale's love of heirlooms blossomed at the age of thirteen, when she purchased her first china cups at an auction. Fostering Olivier's interest was his "passion for Pascale," he quips. Their business evolved from owning several stores to hosting their famed sale at the château and selling at a few fairs in England and Sweden.

The Gisclards' passion for their work and their thrill at unearthing rare pieces translated into an unforgettable experience for all who had the good fortune to visit their legendary sale. Carried far and wide, glittering treasures once purchased at Le Grillon Voyageur now gleam on distant shores.

Opposite: Layers of beauty can be observed in a lush bouquet topping a vintage Swedish chest, below left, and in a view from the dining room to the front entry, above left. This page: Graceful details highlight a shapely Vieux Paris coffee service.

Splendor of Christmas | 89

A rustic eighteenth-century French window has been repurposed as a mirror, above left, and a grouping of old picture frames complements a hand-painted mercury glass vase, above right. Opposite: The Gisclards curated the diminutive nineteenth-century Swedish table and made the one-of-a-kind chandelier.

90 | Splendor of Christmas

"Searching for antiques is full of surprises that never come twice," says Olivier Gisclard. "With new people, places, and objects, you keep learning every day." Opposite: A glimpse indoors from the garden reveals an enchanting tableau. This page, clockwise from above left: Etched glass liqueur bottles from Sweden and a collection of French keys, a lovely British tea set, and a Christmas tree adorned with handmade paper ornaments offer lovely vignettes.

Splendor of Christmas | 93

AN ESCAPE TO PARIS

Amid towering trees draped in ribbons and baubles, charming markets, and sounds of children laughing as they glide about ice rinks or spin on singing carousels, Paris is aglow in rich traditions of Christmas. A wintertime sojourn to this luminescent capital city enchants with iconic sites dressed in holiday trimmings.

Opposite: At Place Vendôme, a fashionable square in Paris that is home to luxury retailers such as jeweler Van Cleef & Arpels, towering evergreens lend holiday cheer to an afternoon of Christmas shopping. This page, above: Delicate orbs twinkle above the festive and bright offerings of a local florist.

Against the chilly silhouette of a winter night, the City of Light is never brighter than at Yuletide. By mid-November, the first harbingers of holiday magic appear: a whisper of tinsel and a twinkle of bulbs in the branches. Soon, like a snuggly wound scarf, all of Paris is enveloped in the spirit of Christmas.

While a shopping spree is always fruitful in Paris, annual window displays make the activity even more eye-catching. In 1893, Le Bon Marché, one of Europe's oldest department stores, fashioned a scene of graceful skaters gliding across a frozen pond, but in 1909, the company hired a mechanical dollmaker to render a miniature interpretation of Commodore Robert Peary's North Pole expedition. Ever since, locales from Galeries Lafayette to Printemps Haussmann unveil theatrical displays complete with interactive figurines—a tradition growing in spectacle each year, as friendly competition spurs greater unveilings.

Beyond large emporiums, wooden chalets cluster in the streets, overflowing with charming trinkets and tasty treats. Wander between booths sipping on *vin chaud*, a warming mulled wine, in pursuit of artisan gifts.

When feet grow weary from perusing treasures and munching roasted chestnuts, there is no shortage of hotels and eateries waiting to host with festive trimmings and holiday pastries. Enjoy a cozy Christmas brew in Salon Proust at The Ritz, or sip steaming hot chocolate at iconic Parisian teahouse Angelina.

By the first weeks of January, glitz and glamour are packed away until next year, but between cheery showcases and heartwarming markets, a Parisian sojourn promises snow-kissed memories to tuck deep in one's heart.

Clockwise from center left: Fashion and ballet mingle in the window display of Repetto, while cocoa confections and holiday cheer entice patrons to visit À La Mère de Famille. Angelina's ethereal pastries take on a seasonal aesthetic in December. Constructed in 1823, the ornate arches and mosaic floors of Galerie Vivienne pave the path to luxury shopping. Following yearly tradition, a grand Christmas tree stretches its faux branches to the skylight of Galeries Lafayette as a cascade of ornaments and ribbons flows to the floor. Opposite: An institution in Parisian culture and the birthplace of the double-shell macaron, Ladurée dresses its windows and overhangs with colorful baubles and greenery, with a lighted bow adding the final grace note.

Amid the hustle and bustle of Yuletide shopping and the chill of snowy weather swirling outside the window, the Ritz Paris offers an elegant teatime experience at Salon Proust. Named for beloved French novelist Marcel Proust—who loyally wined and dined at the hotel, observing patrons who inspired characters in his novels—the space is tinged with literary soul. Belle Epoque furnishings and antique bookshelves offer a dreamy backdrop to enjoy decadent offerings. Sample signature glazed madeleines or a special Christmas treat paired with a classic warm brew.

A fanciful decorative swan crowns a display of holiday wares at Ladurée, above left, while brilliant garlands and a resplendent butterfly welcome patrons to Dior, above right. Opposite: In between perusing treasures and sipping hot chocolate at the Tuileries Garden Christmas Market, a bright carousel offers a moment of whimsy.

Splendor of Christmas | 105

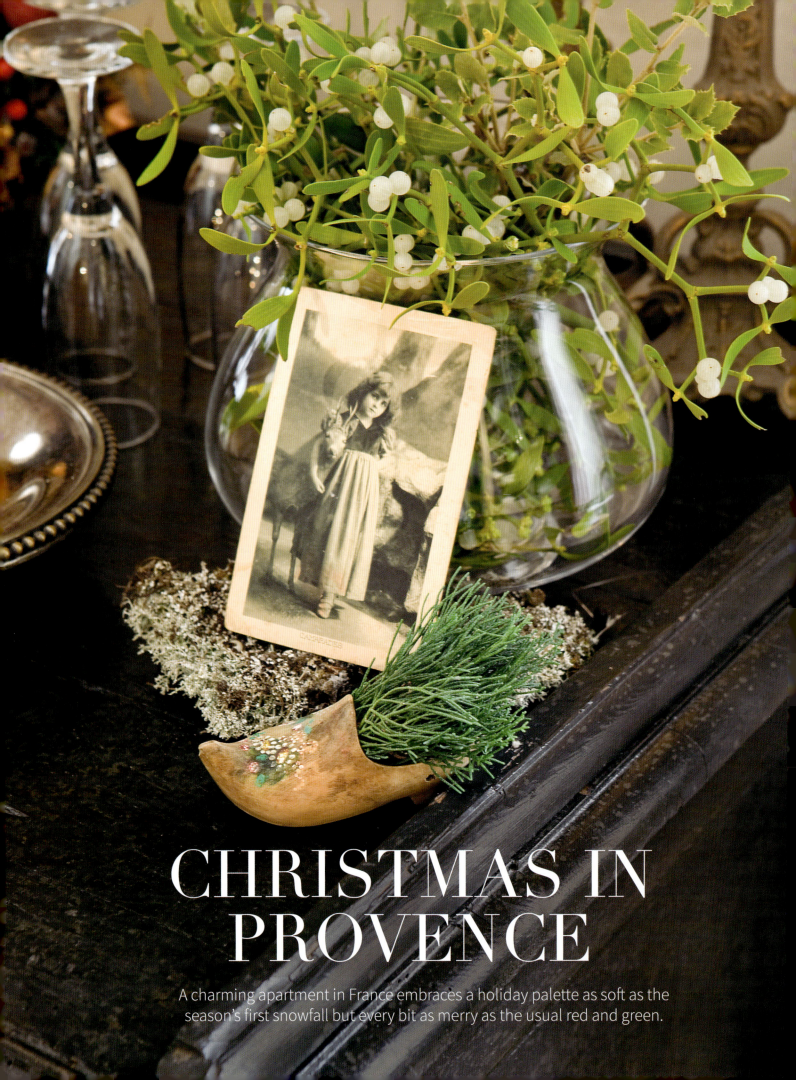

CHRISTMAS IN PROVENCE

A charming apartment in France embraces a holiday palette as soft as the season's first snowfall but every bit as merry as the usual red and green.

The living room ceiling soars to an impressive height, drawing eyes to the unique woodwork. Original patterned parquet floors lend both texture and interest, while a jasmine-vine wreath offers a hint of Christmas.

Splendor of Christmas | 107

> *"WHEN DECORATING THIS APARTMENT FOR CHRISTMAS, I TRIED TO KEEP IT TRADITIONAL AND CLASSIC."*
> —Corey Amaro

Christmas truly is a celebration in Provence, with vibrant holiday markets, miles of fairy lights, and crèches displayed throughout this popular region of France. Beginning with the Feast of Sainte Barbe on December 4 and continuing into the new year, the period the French call Calendales is a joyous time focused on family togetherness.

In a setting that could be mistaken for a Cézanne landscape painting come to life, the community of Apt rests between the mountains of Luberon and Vaucluse. This quintessential Provençal town abounds with centuries-old residences that shine their brightest this time of year, and the beautiful seventeenth-century apartment owned by antiques dealers Nathalie and Jean-Bernard Masset is a perfect example.

"They lovingly, completely renovated it themselves, removing hundreds of years of plaster and taking it back to the original stone walls and wood ceiling," explains stylist Corey Amaro. She enhanced the gracious interiors with seasonal décor befitting the home's Continental chic and historical ambience.

A faded postcard of a young girl, her arm encircling a deer, is typical of the charming vintage accents Corey used to imbue the quarters with subtle touches of the Christmas spirit. Since French tradition calls for children to leave not stockings but shoes for Père Noël to fill, she arranged several captivating vignettes that feature antique wooden clogs. She also turned to nature for inspiration, gathering mistletoe and moss from the nearby Provençal foothills and clipping jasmine from the Massets' garden for fresh-cut wreaths and arrangements.

The metallic hues of gold, silver, and icy blue underscore the aura of elegance, also creating a festive atmosphere that is the hallmark of Christmastide. While it's often easy to overdo Yuletide decorations, Corey has erred on the side of simplicity, making a much more poignant statement.

Splendor of Christmas | 109

Stylist Corey Amaro collected moss from nearby hills and combined the velvety tufts with mercury glass balls and candles in order to compose pretty arrangements on the coffee table and across the mantel. As daylight fades to evening, this conversation area takes on a gentle glow that encourages loved ones to linger in the space.

Splendor of Christmas | 111

"CHRISTMAS IN FRANCE IS MORE ABOUT BEING TOGETHER AS A FAMILY AND CELEBRATING WITH A BEAUTIFUL MEAL."
—Corey Amaro

Opposite: Sprigs of mistletoe stand in pharmacy bottles from the early 1900s. This page: Lit candles offer a mesmerizing glow.

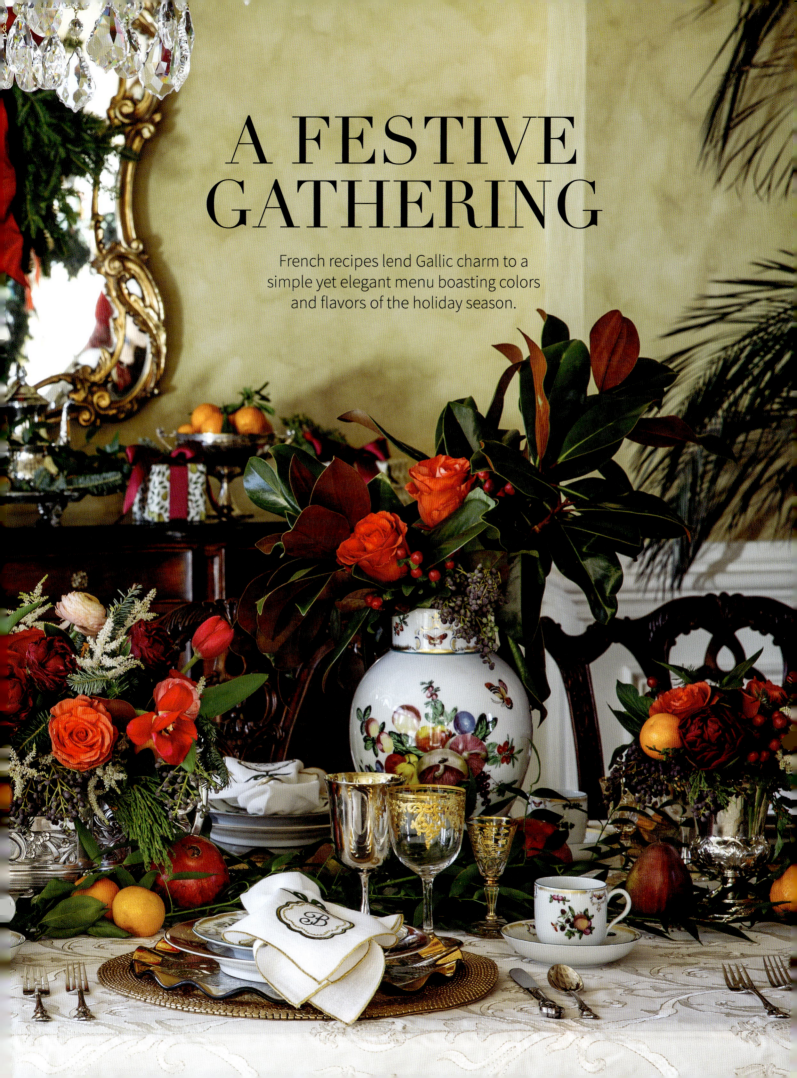

A FESTIVE GATHERING

French recipes lend Gallic charm to a simple yet elegant menu boasting colors and flavors of the holiday season.

Opposite: Setting the scene for this elegant affair is Mottahedeh Duke of Gloucester china. Comprising twenty colors and 22-karat gold, the stunning pattern offers a grand tribute to Rococo style, with an exuberant gathering of fruits forming the center medallion and other natural motifs lending charm to colorful borders. This page: Citrus and bloom unite in arrangements that enhance the tableau.

Splendor of Christmas | 119

Opposite: Dinner opens with the satisfying mingling of textures in Smoked Salmon Sesame Crisps. Here, whipped crème fraîche and citrus-kissed fish meet on a homemade cracker. This page, above right: The balance continues with Haricots Verts Amandine. Next spread: Completing the menu are comforting Gratin Dauphinois and Poulet au Vinaigre, a bistro dish of tender braised chicken with vinegar sauce.

120 | Splendor of Christmas

Splendor of Christmas | 123

According to legend, the iconic Bûche de Noël takes its inspiration from the long-ago Celtic tradition of burning a freshly cut Yule log in celebration of the winter solstice. Our version of the treat features a spiced chocolate sponge cake brushed generously with cranberry simple syrup and wrapped into a spiral with a decadent filling of vanilla bean buttercream. Shaped into a natural form, the confection comes to life with a combination of chocolate shards and buttercream creating a bark-like appearance. Sugared cranberries, meringue mushrooms, and garnishes of confectioners' sugar, crushed pistachios, and fresh rosemary add the final touches to this noteworthy dessert.

RECIPE INDEX

chives, lemon zest, lemon juice, and pepper. Cover and refrigerate until ready to use.
6. In a medium bowl, beat cream with a mixer or by hand until soft peaks form; add crème fraîche and beat until medium peaks form. Cover and refrigerate until ready to use.
7. Right before serving, spoon salmon onto sesame crisps and top with whipped crème fraîche. Garnish with capers, if desired, and serve immediately.

Poulet au Vinaigre
Makes 4 to 6 servings

1 (2½- to 3-pound) **chicken**, cut into 10 pieces
1 tablespoon **kosher salt**, divided
1 teaspoon ground **black pepper**, divided
1 tablespoon **olive oil**
½ cup minced **shallot**
2 teaspoons sliced **garlic**
1 cup seeded, diced **plum tomato**
1 cup **low-sodium chicken broth**
1 cup **dry white wine**
½ cup **white wine vinegar**
1 tablespoon **honey**
2 tablespoons **water**
1 tablespoon **cornstarch**
2 tablespoons **unsalted butter**, cubed
2 teaspoons chopped fresh **tarragon**
2 tablespoons chopped fresh **parsley**
Garnish: **tarragon sprigs**

Smoked Salmon Sesame Crisps
Makes approximately 6 servings

2½ tablespoons **unsalted butter**, softened
½ cup **confectioners' sugar**
⅓ cup **bread flour**
½ teaspoon **kosher salt**
1 large **egg white**
1 teaspoon **white sesame seeds**
1 teaspoon **black sesame seeds**
3 ounces **smoked salmon**, finely chopped
2 teaspoons finely minced **shallot**
1 teaspoon chopped **chives**
½ teaspoon **lemon zest**
1 teaspoon **lemon juice**
⅛ teaspoon ground **black pepper**
½ cup **heavy whipping cream**
¼ cup **crème fraîche**
Garnish: drained **capers**

1. Preheat oven to 350°. Using a permanent marker and a 1½-inch round cutter as a guide, draw circles at least 1½ inches apart on a sheet of parchment paper; slide template under a nonstick baking mat on a baking sheet.
2. In a stand mixer fitted with the paddle attachment, beat butter, confectioners' sugar, bread flour, and salt at low speed until smooth. Add egg white and mix at low speed until incorporated. Cover and refrigerate until firm, 30 minutes.
3. Spoon ½ teaspoon batter into each circle on prepared pan. Using an offset spatula, thinly spread paste evenly inside circle. Sprinkle with sesame seeds.
4. Bake until edges are golden brown, 6 to 8 minutes. Let cool completely on a wire rack.
5. In a small bowl, combine salmon, shallot,

1. Preheat oven to 325°.
2. Pat chicken dry with paper towels, and sprinkle with 2 teaspoons kosher salt. Refrigerate, uncovered, until salt is absorbed, at least 1 hour. Remove from refrigerator and sprinkle with ½ teaspoon pepper.
3. In a 12-inch braiser, heat olive oil over medium-high heat. Add chicken, skin side down; cook until browned, 3 to 5 minutes per side. Remove from pan; pour off all but 2 tablespoons drippings.
4. Reduce heat to medium. Add shallot, garlic, remaining 1 teaspoon salt, and remaining ½ teaspoon pepper; cook, stirring constantly, until fragrant, 1 minute. Stir in tomatoes and cook, stirring frequently, until tomatoes break down, 3 to 5 minutes. Add broth, wine,

RECIPE INDEX

vinegar, and honey; simmer, scraping bottom of braiser with a wooden spoon. Return chicken to braiser, skin side up.

5. Bake, uncovered, until chicken is cooked through, 35 to 40 minutes. Remove chicken to serving platter.

6. In a small bowl, whisk 2 tablespoons water with cornstarch.

7. Bring cooking liquid to a boil over medium-high heat. Whisk in cornstarch mixture. Cook, stirring occasionally, until reduced by half, 10 to 15 minutes. While whisking constantly, drop cubed butter, 1 cube at a time, into sauce, until butter is melted and sauce is smooth. Remove from heat and stir in tarragon. Pour sauce around chicken, top with parsley, and serve. Garnish with tarragon sprigs, if desired.

Haricots Verts Amandine
Makes 4 to 6 servings

- 1 tablespoon plus ½ teaspoon **kosher salt**, divided
- 1 pound **French green beans**, trimmed
- ¼ cup sliced **almonds**
- 3 tablespoons **unsalted butter**
- ¼ cup thinly sliced **shallots**
- 2 teaspoons sliced **garlic**
- 2 tablespoons fresh **lemon juice**
- ¼ teaspoon ground **black pepper**
- Garnish: toasted sliced **almonds**, **lemon zest**

1. Bring a large pot of water to a boil over medium-high heat; add 1 tablespoon salt and haricots verts. Cook until crisp-tender, about 2 minutes. Drain and immediately place in ice water; drain again and place in a large bowl.

2. In a large, dry skillet, toast almonds over medium heat, stirring frequently, until golden and fragrant, 3 to 5 minutes. Remove to bowl.

3. In same pan, melt butter over medium heat until butter turns lightly golden. Add shallots and garlic; cook, stirring constantly, until fragrant, 1 to 2 minutes. Whisk in lemon juice, pepper, and remaining ½ teaspoon salt. Toss in green beans and almonds; cook until heated through.

4. Spoon into serving bowl. Garnish with toasted almonds and lemon zest, if desired.

Gratin Dauphinois
Makes approximately 8 servings

- 2 tablespoons **unsalted butter**, divided
- ¾ cup grated **yellow onion**
- 3 teaspoons grated **garlic**
- 3 teaspoons **kosher salt**
- 1½ teaspoons freshly ground **black pepper**
- ⅜ teaspoon freshly ground **nutmeg**
- 4½ cups **heavy whipping cream**
- 1½ cups **whole milk**
- 3¾ pounds **Yukon gold potatoes**, peeled and sliced ⅛-inch thick
- 6 **thyme sprigs**
- 3 **bay leaves**
- 3 tablespoons **cornstarch**
- 1¼ cups shredded **Gruyère cheese**
- Garnish: **thyme leaves**

1. Preheat oven to 350°. Butter a 13x9-inch baking dish with 1 tablespoon butter.

2. In a large Dutch oven, melt remaining 1 tablespoon butter over medium heat. Add onion and cook until tender, 3 to 5 minutes. Stir in garlic, salt, pepper, and nutmeg; cook, stirring constantly, until fragrant, 1 minute. Stir in cream, milk, potatoes, thyme sprigs, and bay leaves. Bring to a boil; reduce heat and simmer until potatoes begin to soften, about 8 minutes. Remove from heat.

3. Drain potatoes over a bowl, reserving 2⅔ cups cooking liquid. Let potatoes cool for 20 minutes. Discard thyme and bay leaves. Arrange potatoes in prepared pan in overlapping, fanned rows. Whisk cornstarch into reserved cooking liquid; pour over potatoes until potatoes are mostly covered. Sprinkle with cheese.

4. Cover and bake until sauce is thick and bubbly, about 25 minutes. Uncover and continue to bake until cheese is lightly browned, 20 to 25 minutes more. Let cool for 15 minutes before serving. Garnish with thyme, if desired.

Bûche de Noël
Makes 1 cake

- 4 large **eggs**, room temperature
- ¾ cup **granulated sugar**
- 1 teaspoon **vanilla bean paste**
- ¾ cup **all-purpose flour**
- ¼ cup **Dutch process cocoa powder***, plus more for dusting
- 1 tablespoon **cornstarch**
- 1 teaspoon **baking powder**
- 1 teaspoon ground **cinnamon**
- ½ teaspoon ground **ginger**
- ½ teaspoon **kosher salt**
- ¼ teaspoon ground **nutmeg**
- ⅓ cup **sour cream**, room temperature
- ¼ cup **vegetable oil**
- 4 ounces **60% bittersweet chocolate**, chopped
- 2 teaspoons **coconut oil**
- **Sugared Cranberries with Simple Syrup** (recipe follows)
- **Vanilla Bean Buttercream** (recipe follows)
- **Chocolate Buttercream** (recipe follows)
- **Meringue Mushrooms** (recipe follows)
- Garnish: ground **pistachios**, fresh **rosemary**, **confectioners' sugar**

1. Preheat oven to 350°. Spray a 17½x12½ rimmed baking sheet with baking spray with flour. Line pan with parchment paper; spray parchment.

2. In the bowl of a stand mixer fitted with the whisk attachment, beat eggs and granulated sugar at high speed until thick and pale, 5 to 7 minutes. Beat in vanilla bean paste.

3. In a medium bowl, sift together flour, cocoa, cornstarch, baking powder, cinnamon, ginger, salt, and nutmeg. Gently fold flour mixture into egg mixture.

4. In a small bowl, whisk together sour cream and vegetable oil. Fold sour cream mixture into egg mixture, scraping bottom of bowl to fully combine. Spread batter into prepared pan, smoothing top with an offset spatula.

5. Heavily dust a tea towel with cocoa.

6. Bake until set and top springs back when touched, 10 to 12 minutes. Immediately run a sharp knife around edges of pan to loosen cake. Turn out cake onto prepared tea towel. Gently peel off parchment. Starting with one long side, roll up cake and towel together. Let cool completely on a wire rack.

7. Line a baking sheet with a silicone baking mat or parchment paper.

8. In the top of a double boiler, combine chocolate and coconut oil. Cook over simmering water, stirring occasionally, until melted and smooth. Remove from heat.

Pour over prepared pan. Using an offset spatula, spread chocolate mixture in a thin, even layer. Refrigerate until firm.

9. Carefully unroll cake and brush with Simple Syrup from Sugared Cranberries. Spread Vanilla Bean Buttercream on top. Reroll cake without towel, and place, seam side down, on a baking sheet, using towel as a sling. Cover with towel, and refrigerate until firm, about 1 hour.

10. Trim ends of cake flat. Trim 3 to 4 inches diagonally from one end; set aside. Trim a ¾-inch slice from same end; set aside.

11. Place large cut piece at an angle off side of cake, and attach with Chocolate Buttercream. Place small cut piece, angling cut side up, on top, and attach with buttercream. Spread remaining buttercream on outside of cake. Remove chocolate sheet from refrigerator. Using parchment paper, gently crush chocolate to form long shards. Carefully place shards on buttercream to create a bark pattern. Decorate with Meringue Mushrooms and Sugared Cranberries; garnish with pistachios, rosemary, and confectioners' sugar, if desired.

*We used Droste.

Sugared Cranberries with Simple Syrup
Makes ½ cup

¾ cup **granulated sugar**, divided
¼ cup **water**
1 tablespoon **light corn syrup**
½ cup fresh or frozen **cranberries**, thawed

1. In a large saucepan, combine ¼ cup sugar, ¼ cup water, and corn syrup. Bring to a gentle boil over medium heat, and cook until sugar is dissolved and mixture is the consistency of maple syrup, about 10 minutes. Add cranberries and remove from heat (to prevent cranberries from bursting). Gently stir to coat; let cool in syrup.
2. Line a rimmed baking sheet with parchment paper. Drain cranberries, reserving syrup. Roll in remaining ½ cup sugar and place on prepared pan. Let stand until dry, 1 to 2 hours. Cranberries may be stored for 2 days in an airtight container.

Vanilla Bean Buttercream
Makes 3 cups

3 **egg whites**, room temperature
1 cup **granulated sugar**
1¼ cups **unsalted butter**, cubed and softened
1 teaspoon **vanilla bean paste**
¼ teaspoon **kosher salt**

1. In the bowl of a stand mixer, whisk together egg whites and sugar by hand. Place bowl over a saucepan of simmering water. Cook, whisking occasionally, until an instant-read thermometer registers 155° to 160°.
2. Carefully return bowl to stand mixer fitted with the whisk attachment, and beat at high speed until bowl is cool to the touch, about 8 minutes. Add butter, 2 tablespoons at a time, beating until combined after each addition. Beat in vanilla bean paste and salt. Use immediately or refrigerate in an airtight container for up to 3 days. If refrigerating, let stand at room temperature for 2 hours and rewhip until smooth before using.

Chocolate Buttercream
Makes 2 cups

½ cup **unsalted butter**, softened
3 tablespoons **Dutch process cocoa powder***
⅓ cup **sour cream**
2½ cups **confectioners' sugar**

In the bowl of a stand mixer fitted with the paddle attachment, beat butter at medium speed until smooth and creamy, about 2 minutes. Add cocoa, beating until combined. Beat in sour cream until smooth. Gradually add confectioners' sugar, beating until smooth and creamy. Use immediately or refrigerate in an airtight container for up to 3 days. If refrigerating, let stand at room temperature for 2 hours before using.

*We used Droste.

Meringue Mushrooms
Makes 24

2 **egg whites**
¼ teaspoon **cream of tartar**
⅛ teaspoon **kosher salt**
½ cup **granulated sugar**
¼ cup **dark chocolate melting wafers**, melted according to package directions and cooled slightly
Cocoa powder, for dusting

1. Preheat oven to 275°. Line a rimmed baking sheet with parchment paper.
2. In the bowl of a stand mixer fitted with the whisk attachment, beat egg whites, cream of tartar, and salt at low speed until foamy. With mixer at high speed, add sugar in a slow, steady stream. Beat until stiff peaks form.
3. Place meringue in a large piping bag fitted with a ½-inch round tip. Holding tip perpendicular to parchment paper, pipe half of meringue as mushroom tops, ¾ to 1¼ inches across. (Use a wet finger to press down any points.) With remaining meringue, pipe stems as large kisses with ½-inch-wide base. (It is OK if the kisses don't have smooth tips.)
4. Bake until meringues look dry and have started to brown slightly, 30 to 40 minutes. Let cool completely.
5. Using a wooden pick, poke a small hole in bottom of each mushroom top. Dip or brush melted chocolate on bottom of each mushroom top, and insert pointed stem end. Let stand until chocolate is set, about 5 minutes. Lightly dust with cocoa before serving. Mushrooms are best served the same day.

A FAIRY-TALE FARMHOUSE

As gingerbread bakes in the oven and tiny lights are strewn about the home, a Gallic dwelling enriched with the spirit of Yuletide is an idyllic haven in which to spend the holidays.

Above left and opposite: Though the air is crisp, an outdoor table Marlies scavenged from one of the property's sheds sets a cozy scene outside of the farm's main entrance. Readied for afternoon refreshment with glasses of wine and light bites, plush blankets keep one warm as conversations linger into the evening. Antique ornaments and greenery embellished with antlers are from the couple's web shop, where they sell *brocante* market finds.

Tucked deep into the hearts of many is a dream of owning a second home in the French countryside. For one Dutch couple, Marlies and Ralph, years of family vacations to this beloved land, where rolling hills lead the way to pastures of grazing sheep and cattle, prompted the pair to ask themselves, why not find a place to call their own?

After a deep scouring of listings in search of the one that met the yearning in their souls, they found it: a thoughtfully maintained farm in the Cher province. In addition, with the reasonable price and ideal driving distance from their primary residence in the Netherlands, the property possessed everything they searched for: a peaceful ambience, unparalleled views, charming patina, and even an old pigsty that could be converted into a guesthouse.

It is easy to see why Marlies was immediately captivated by the space as, luckily, the previous owner kept the farmhouse in excellent condition. All that was needed was a fresh coat of chalk paint to ready the dwelling for touches of her personal taste. "Interiors and styling have always been my passion, and I have always had a predilection for *brocantes*," Marlies says. It is fortuitous that the property is nearby a wealth of flea markets and antiques shops. Upon each visit, new treasures are collected for both of the couple's residences and to sell via an online shop.

At Yuletide, a special holiday magic drapes over the scenery. The table is set with festive chinaware from Rivièra Maison, and swaths of greenery are tucked throughout interiors and exteriors. "We find it beautiful here in the winter months," Marlies says. The homeowners opt to spend Christmas here every year. Time loses its hold as they gather with loved ones, cradled in the serene embrace of their created paradise.

Opposite: With an authentic stone floor providing earthy color cues, the main dining area exudes a soothing aura. A table discovered from an online marketplace was sanded, painted, and treated with a matte finish. The wood stove is original to the house, providing warmth in winter months. When Yuletide arrives, Marlies visits a local garden center to gather masses of greenery, festooning the abode with festive layers.

Clockwise from above left: When the couple acquired the farmhouse, a few pieces came with the purchase, including a wooden armoire in the primary bedroom. Echoing the deep tones of the wardrobe, a French bed was added and dressed in soft linens from the homeowners' shop. Tiny votives add glimmers of romantic light throughout the interiors, calling to mind Christmases of bygone days. An antique desk perches in the corner near a tall window so that the morning sun may offer its bright rays for the task of penning holiday correspondence. A vintage typewriter is a charming accessory to the writing table, filled with fresh paper for holiday missives.

As frost creeps over the windowpanes, a pair of leather armchairs creates a cozy nook for reading a novel or sipping a glass of wine with a loved one. At first, Ralph thought the wingbacks too worn, but Marlies convinced him they possess a unique beauty.

Splendor of Christmas | 137

PARFUM, MON AMOUR

Like peering at the magical scene within a snow globe, the windows of a perfumery offer an enticing peek at shimmering displays inside.

Ernest Daltroff established legendary French perfumery The House of Caron in 1904, and though he had no formal training as a perfumer, he inherited a love of fragrance from his mother. He also possessed a discriminating sense of smell, commonly known in the business as having a "nose." Two years after the company's creation, former dressmaker Félicie Wanpouille joined the staff, contributing her creative talents to eye-catching bottle designs—and winning Ernest's heart in the process. Together, they composed a number of Caron's iconic scents, including N'Aimez que Moi, which translates to "love no one but me." The pair also counted Tabac Blond and Pour un Homme among their classic collaborations.

Through the years, Caron has enjoyed an esteemed position in the world of perfumeries. At its height of success, the brand grew to include four boutiques—three in Paris and one in New York City, offering the very picture of opulence. The former Rue du Faubourg Saint-Honoré location, which opened in 2000, gleamed with beautiful marble tables, lion's-paw consoles, and an array of gold-trimmed Baccarat and Daum crystal fountains dispensing the brand's ambrosial products. A collection of refillable bottles lining the shelves of a backlit glass case created a fitting display for these true works of art.

Caron's tradition of memorable offerings continues with perfumes available through fine retailers around the world, as well at the company's Paris boutique at 23 Rue François. Perhaps, if a lady wishes hard enough, she might discover a bottle of an exclusive scent, such as classic Fleurs de Rocaille, wrapped in the company's signature gold dots and silky ribbon, beneath her Christmas tree.

Situated opposite the Élysée Palace, which serves as the official residence of the president of France, the former Rue du Faubourg Saint-Honoré boutique displays unique crystal fountains. Caron's coveted fragrances can still be found in the 8th arrondissement at the Rue François location.

Revolutionary in its vision for a "Haute Parfumerie," the brand's groundbreaking approach has garnered many achievements, including several firsts: exploring leathery notes, introducing men's fragrance, and offering refillable bottles. Visiting a boutique affords the opportunity to connect with a Caron ambassador, who can guide patrons through a private consultation, fill bottles at a perfume fountain, and personalize gifts.

A SIDEBOARD OF SWEET TEMPTATIONS

A softly illuminated room contributes to an old-world feel. This refined spread, in a courtly French setting, presents the perfect opportunity to announce the season. And it is a wonderful way to toast friendships old and new.

"COME QUICKLY! FOR I AM DRINKING THE STARS."

—Dom Pérignon,
upon the discovery of Champagne

One of the architects of the most reputable salons was the Marquise de Rambouillet, a woman of letters admired for her social skills and graces. So popular were her gatherings that her home became known as the Hôtel de Rambouillet, described in *Brewer's Dictionary of Phrase and Fable* as "the reunion of rank and literary genius on terms of equality; a coterie where sparkling wit and polished manners prevail."

To create your own salon-like gathering, first consider your guests. An adept mix of people will ensure lively and pleasant discourse on a range of topics, from the social to the serious. To help uncork the flow of sparkling conversation among guests, serve chilled Champagne, perhaps coffee and espresso, and an assortment of light bites.

Delicious morsels encourage guests to indulge in two of the loveliest delights to be shared among amiable companions: dessert and repartee. Below, we offer Chocolate Toffee Truffles; Tartes de Linz; Chocolate, Cherry, and Hazelnut Terrine; Mini Pear Galettes; and Buttermilk–Grand Marnier Panna Cotta.

RECIPE INDEX

Pumpkin Chai Pots de Crème
Makes 12 servings

1½ cups **whole milk**
½ cup canned **pumpkin**
¼ cup **granulated sugar**
¼ cup firmly packed **light brown sugar**
1 teaspoon **vanilla extract**
¼ teaspoon ground **cloves**
¼ teaspoon ground **ginger**
¼ teaspoon ground **cinnamon**
⅛ teaspoon ground **nutmeg**
⅛ teaspoon **salt**
10 **egg yolks**
Garnish: **sweetened whipped cream**, crumbled **pistachios**

1. Preheat oven to 325°.
2. In a small saucepan, combine milk, pumpkin, granulated sugar, brown sugar, vanilla extract, cloves, ginger, cinnamon, nutmeg, and salt over medium heat. Whisk to combine. Just as mixture begins to boil, remove from heat.
3. In a small bowl, whisk egg yolks. Stir yolks into hot milk mixture, a little at a time. Strain mixture through a fine-mesh sieve, discarding solids.
4. Evenly divide mixture among 12 (2-ounce) espresso cups. Place cups in a large baking dish. Pour enough water into baking dish to come halfway up sides of cups.
5. Bake until custards are set, except for a dime-size portion in center, 40 to 45 minutes. Remove from oven, and let cool in baking dish for 30 minutes.
6. Remove cups from pan, and wrap with plastic wrap, being careful not to let plastic touch surface of custard. Refrigerate for at least 4 hours and up to 2 days. Before serving, garnish with whipped cream and pistachios, if desired.

Chocolate, Cherry, and Hazelnut Terrine
Makes approximately 80 confections

1½ cups **cocoa powder**
1 cup **unsalted butter**, softened
9 ounces **bittersweet chocolate**, melted
1 cup **granulated sugar**
½ cup **water**
2 large **eggs**
3 **egg yolks**
¼ cup **amaretto liqueur**
2 cups crushed **vanilla wafers**
1 cup **hazelnuts**, toasted
½ cup **dried cherries**

1. Lightly spray a 10-inch loaf pan with cooking spray.
2. In the bowl of a stand mixer, beat cocoa powder and butter at medium speed until fluffy. Add melted chocolate and continue beating to combine.
3. In a small saucepan, bring sugar and ½ cup water to a boil. Cook simple syrup until mixture registers 220° on a candy thermometer. With mixer running at low speed, add simple syrup to chocolate mixture in a slow, steady stream, beating until combined.
4. In a small bowl, whisk together eggs, egg yolks, and liqueur. Add egg mixture to hot chocolate mixture, and beat to combine well. Using a spatula, fold in wafers, hazelnuts, and cherries.
5. Evenly spread mixture in prepared pan. (Tap pan on counter to release any air bubbles.) Cover pan tightly with plastic wrap, and refrigerate until set, at least 4 hours.
6. To unmould, place bottom one-third of pan into warm water for about 20 seconds to loosen. Invert terrine onto a cutting board. (If top and sides are too soft, refrigerate to stiffen.)
7. Using a serrated knife, carefully cut loaf into ½-inch-thick slices. Cut each slice diagonally into quarters. Refrigerate in an airtight container for up to 2 days.

Mini Pear Galettes
Makes approximately 12

3 cups **all-purpose flour**
⅓ cup plus 1 tablespoon **granulated sugar**, divided
¼ teaspoon **salt**
⅔ cup cold **unsalted butter**, cut into cubes
⅓ cup **ice water**, strained
¾ cup **pear preserves**
2 **egg yolks**
¼ cup **heavy whipping cream**
¼ cup **sliced almonds**

1. In the work bowl of a food processor, add flour, ⅓ cup sugar, and salt; pulse to combine. Add butter and pulse until mixture is crumbly. With processor running at medium speed, pour ⅓ cup ice-cold water through food chute in a slow, steady stream until dough comes together and forms a ball.
2. Remove dough and wrap with plastic wrap. Refrigerate for 2 to 4 hours.
3. Preheat oven to 350°. Line 2 baking sheets with parchment paper.
4. On a lightly floured work surface, roll dough to ¼-inch thickness. Using a 4-inch cutter, cut rounds from dough. Gather scraps, and roll once more, cutting more rounds. Place approximately 1 tablespoon pear preserves on centers of each round. Roll edge of dough inward, overlapping in a circular pattern. Place galettes on prepared pans.
5. In a small bowl, whisk together egg yolks and cream. Brush galettes with egg mixture, and sprinkle evenly with remaining 1 tablespoon sugar and almonds.
6. Bake until golden brown, 35 to 40 minutes. Serve warm. Cover and refrigerate for up to 1 day.

Tartes de Linz
Makes approximately 14 tarts

½ cup chopped **toasted hazelnuts**
½ cup slivered **toasted almonds**
2⅓ cups **all-purpose flour**, divided
¾ cup firmly packed **light brown sugar**
1 teaspoon ground **cinnamon**
½ teaspoon **baking powder**
½ teaspoon **salt**
½ teaspoon ground **nutmeg**
1 cup cold **unsalted butter**, cubed
3 **egg yolks**
2 teaspoons **vanilla extract**
1 teaspoon **butter extract**
½ cup **cranberry jam**
½ cup **cherry preserves**

1. Preheat oven to 350°. Lightly spray 14 (4-inch) barquette tart pans with cooking spray.
2. In the work bowl of a food processor, combine hazelnuts, almonds, and ⅓ cup flour. Pulse until nuts are finely chopped.
3. Transfer mixture to a large bowl. Add remaining 2 cups flour, brown sugar, cinnamon, baking powder, salt, and nutmeg. Whisk to blend.
4. Add butter and beat with a mixer at low speed until mixture resembles coarse crumbs. Add egg yolks, vanilla extract, and

butter extract; beat just until combined.
5. Gather dough into 2 balls. Wrap 1 ball in plastic wrap, and refrigerate until ready to use. Using remaining dough, divide into 14 balls, and evenly press into bottoms and up sides of prepared pans.
6. In a small bowl, combine cranberry jam and cherry preserves. Evenly divide mixture among tarts.
7. Place remaining dough between 2 sheets of parchment paper; roll into a rectangle approximately 18x7 inches and ¼-inch thick. Freeze rectangle until firm, about 5 minutes.
8. Cut rectangle lengthwise into 14 (½-inch-wide) strips. Cut each 18-inch long strip into 6 (3-inch-long) pieces, for a total of 84 (3x½-inch) strips. Arrange 3 strips diagonally across each tart, spacing evenly. Arrange 3 more strips diagonally across each tart in opposite direction, forming lattice. Seal ends of strips to dough edge, trimming excess.
9. Bake until golden brown, 12 to 15 minutes. Transfer to a wire rack and let cool completely before gently squeezing tart pans to remove Linzer tortes. Store at room temperature for up to 2 days.

Chocolate-Toffee Truffles
Makes approximately 24

¼ cup **heavy whipping cream**
¼ cup **whole milk**
1 tablespoon **English toffee syrup**
6 (1-ounce) squares **bittersweet chocolate**, chopped
4 (1-ounce) squares **milk chocolate**, chopped
1 (8-ounce) bag **toffee chips**, divided

1. In a medium saucepan, combine cream, milk, and toffee syrup over medium heat. Bring to a boil; remove from heat.
2. In a heatproof bowl, combine bittersweet chocolate and milk chocolate. Pour hot cream mixture over chocolate, stirring gently until completely melted. Mix in ½ cup toffee chips.
3. Pour mixture into an airtight container, and refrigerate for at least 1 hour.
4. Using a 1-inch spring-loaded ice cream scoop, scoop chocolate mixture. Roll into 1-inch balls, refrigerating to chill if mixture becomes too soft.
5. Coat truffles with remaining toffee chips. Cover and refrigerate until ready to serve, up to 2 weeks.

Buttermilk–Grand Marnier Panna Cotta
Makes 12 servings

½ cup **buttermilk**
1 (0.25-ounce) envelope **unflavored gelatin**
1 cup **heavy whipping cream**
¼ cup **granulated sugar**
1 tablespoon **orange liqueur**
1 tablespoon **orange zest**
½ **vanilla bean**, split lengthwise
12 rounds **Pistachio Shortbread** (recipe follows)

1. In a small bowl, combine buttermilk and gelatin; let stand until softened, about 2 minutes.
2. In a small saucepan, combine cream, sugar, liqueur, orange zest, and vanilla bean. Bring just to a boil over medium heat; remove from heat.
3. Stir in buttermilk mixture, whisking until all gelatin is dissolved; strain through a fine-mesh sieve into a container or large measuring cup, discarding solids.
4. Divide mixture among 12 (1.75-ounce) silicone moulds. Refrigerate for 4 hours.
5. To unmould, gently pull edges of custards to loosen. Invert onto Pistachio Shortbread rounds, and serve immediately.

Pistachio Shortbread
Makes approximately 24 cookies

⅔ cup **unsalted butter**, softened
1 tablespoon **pistachio paste**
¼ cup **confectioners' sugar**
¼ teaspoon **vanilla extract**
¾ cup **all-purpose flour**
⅛ teaspoon **salt**
¼ cup finely chopped **pistachios**

1. In a large bowl, beat butter, pistachio paste, confectioners' sugar, and vanilla extract with a mixer at medium speed until creamy.
2. In a medium bowl, sift together flour and salt. Slowly add flour mixture to butter mixture, beating at low speed until combined. Fold in chopped pistachios.
3. Remove dough and wrap with plastic wrap. Refrigerate for at least 2 hours and up to overnight.
4. Preheat oven to 350°. Line a baking sheet with parchment paper.
5. On a lightly floured surface, roll dough to ¼-inch thickness. Cut with a 2-inch fluted round cutter. Place on cookie sheet approximately 1 inch apart.
6. Bake until edges of cookies are lightly browned, 10 to 12 minutes. Let cool on pan for 1 minute; remove to wire rack to let cool completely. Store in an airtight container for up to 1 week.

Colonial
SPLENDOR

The warmth of nostalgia burns brightest at Christmastime, whether savored amid the comforts of home or experienced in history-steeped destinations around the United States. Radiant interiors dressed for the season, sojourns to beloved properties, and tables laden with delicious fare demonstrate the richness of American holiday traditions.

A RETURN TO SIMPLER TIMES

The historic village of Williamsburg celebrates the founding of America all year long, but it offers an especially poignant vision during the holiday season, when homes bear the nostalgic look of Christmases past.

An evergreen wreath adorned with a round post bugle hangs above a corner chair. Opposite: An antique cupboard provides the perfect setting for glass-globed candles and festive clove-studded fruits.

Opposite: Christmas bliss extends to this home's parlor, where red holly berries add a cheerful note and clusters of candles ensconced in hurricane lamps lend both light and ambience. This page: Shelves brim with collected crockery, above left, and a tabletop tree makes a cheery window accent, above right.

Splendor of Christmas | 157

"CHRISTMAS! 'TIS THE SEASON FOR KINDLING THE FIRE IN THE HALL, THE GENIAL FLAME OF CHARITY IN THE HEART."
—Washington Irving

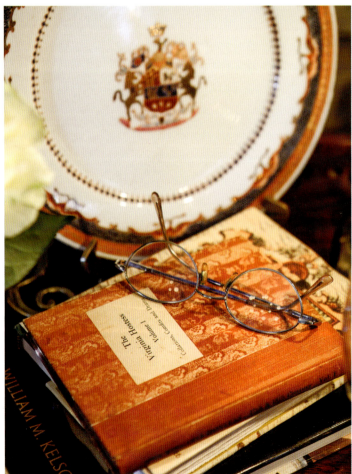

160 | Splendor of Christmas

Opposite: The dining room shimmers with Yuletide brilliance, from the elegantly set table and spectacular tree to the handmade decorations adorning the tableau. This page: Twinkling lights bring sparkle to crystal and silver.

Splendor of Christmas | 163

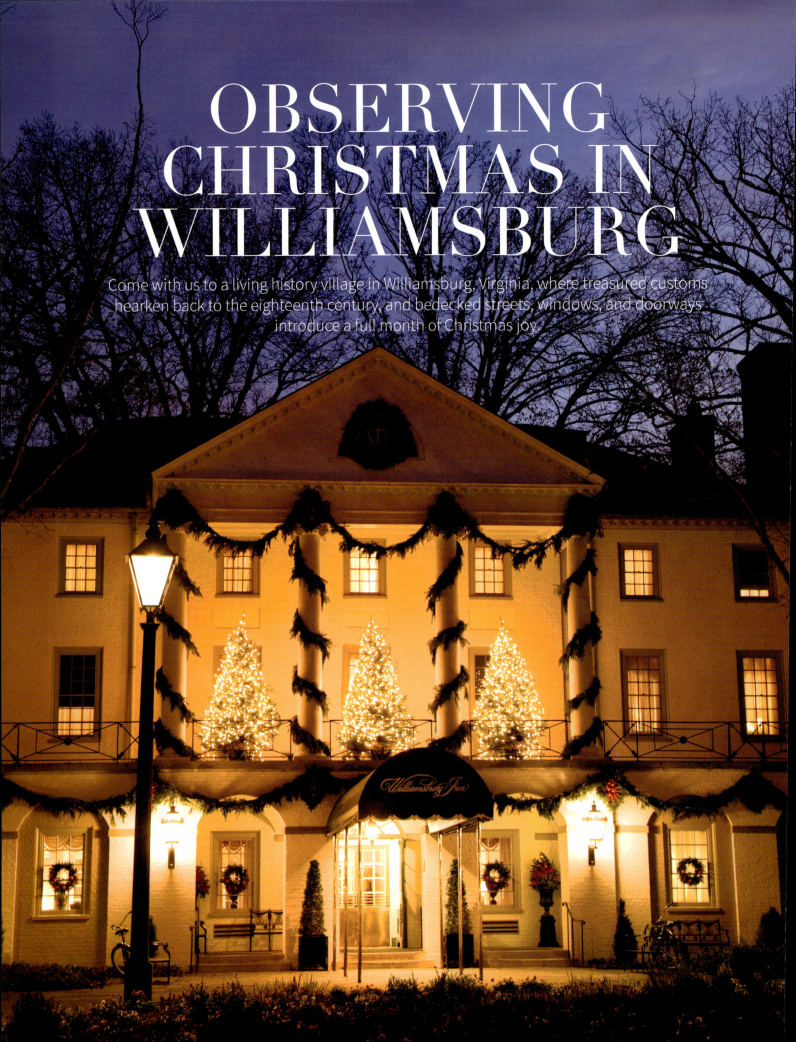

OBSERVING CHRISTMAS IN WILLIAMSBURG

Come with us to a living history village in Williamsburg, Virginia, where treasured customs hearken back to the eighteenth century, and bedecked streets, windows, and doorways introduce a full month of Christmas joy.

As passersby meander through the streets of Colonial Williamsburg's Historic Area at Christmastime, the gaslight lanterns wrapped in evergreen swags and wreaths studded with richly hued fruits and berries seem to whisper a welcome, transporting them to a time when the holiday was a simple yet splendid celebration. During this winter season, the exterior of the Williamsburg Inn is stunningly festive, its windows bathed in a golden glow. Opened in 1937, the establishment was conceived and built by John D. Rockefeller Jr. and his wife, Abby. At Christmas, the premises simply radiate cozy hospitality. The lobby houses a majestic fir tree, decorated with ornaments created by a local miniaturist and topped with a signature Prince of Wales gold crown. Time-honored activities, such as the lighting of the Yule log and storytelling by Father Christmas, are among the holiday traditions celebrated at the inn.

Splendor of Christmas | 165

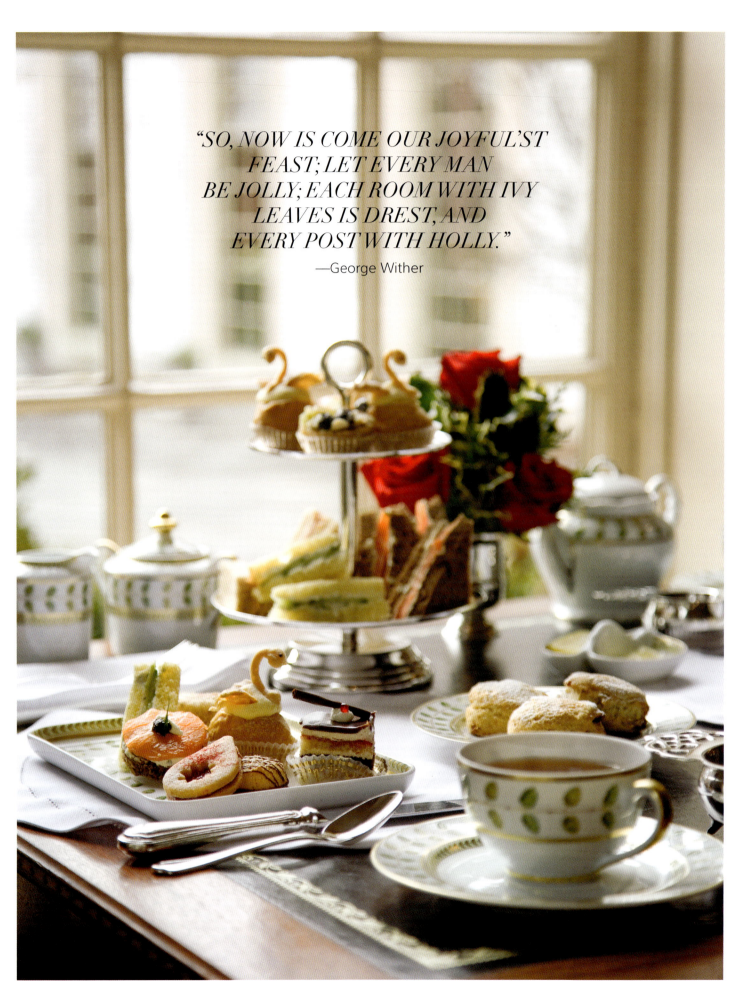

"SO, NOW IS COME OUR JOYFUL'ST FEAST; LET EVERY MAN BE JOLLY; EACH ROOM WITH IVY LEAVES IS DREST, AND EVERY POST WITH HOLLY."

—George Wither

Afternoon tea at the Williamsburg Inn's Terrace Room is a seasonal way to revel in the holiday spirit. Custom-blended teas are paired with epicurean delights, such as warm blueberry scones; finger sandwiches with ham pâté, cucumber and cream cheese, and smoked salmon; fruit tarts, pastry swans filled with crème, and assorted cookies. Tea is served on signature Williamsburg Inn china by Bernardaud and creamware inspired by an eighteenth-century design and manufactured exclusively for Colonial Williamsburg in Leeds, England. The inn's calendar affords special opportunities throughout the year to experience teatime.

During this celebratory time in the 1700s, feasts were varied and plentiful. Nearly every family who was financially able opened their home for a dinnertime gathering. Traditional holiday foods from England—roast beef and goose, plum pudding, and mincemeat pies—were served alongside native wild turkey, duck, venison, and Virginia ham, as well as shrimp, oysters, and many varieties of fish from the nearby waters of the Atlantic. In wealthy households, dinner offerings were surpassed only by the selection and quantity of libations, such as sherry, Madeira, and French brandy. A beautifully decorated table was the focal point of every feast, and hostesses vied for social status through their dessert tables, presented as the grand culmination of a dinner party.

"CHRISTMAS IS COME, HANG ON THE POT, LET SPITS TURN ROUND AND OVENS BE HOT"

—Joseph Royle,
The Virginia Almanac, 1765

All told, the Christmas season lasted twelve days—from Christmas Day through Epiphany on January 6. During this time, homes were filled with neighbors, friends, and family who gathered for parties, dances, and amusements. Virginians most likely followed English custom by adorning their homes and churches with the greenery available during the cold season. Fir and cedar branches, berries, mistletoe, ivy, bay, and other evergreens were bedecked with candles, forced blooms, and even feathers for added texture, color, and light. Holly, with its glossy green leaves and bright red berries, was especially popular, and it featured prominently both indoors and out. Today, Colonial Williamsburg's outdoor Christmas decorations are known worldwide for their use of natural materials available during the eighteenth century. Pine and boxwood wreaths decorated with fresh fruit, nuts, pine cones, and more than 3 miles of white pine roping are used to put the finishing touches on doorways, windows, columns, and railings.

GRAND HOLIDAY ESTATES

From the palatial wonders of a legendary Gilded Age mansion and gardens to the hallowed halls of our first president's home and the welcoming environs of an elegant Southern villa, storied American properties shine their brightest at Yuletide.

Splendor of Christmas | 173

BILTMORE

Constructed at the height of the Gilded Age, Biltmore Estate represents one of the greatest undertakings in the history of American architecture. George W. Vanderbilt, the third son of railroad magnate William Henry Vanderbilt, visited North Carolina frequently with his mother during the 1880s. Smitten with Asheville's majestic scenery and temperate climate, the wealthy heir purchased 125,000 acres and commissioned famed New York City architect Richard Morris Hunt to build a "little mountain escape."

Hunt designed the opulent summer home in the style of working estates in Europe. Inspired by France's Les Châteaux de la Loire, Biltmore is the largest private residence in the United States. The sprawling 4-acre, 250-room mansion took more than six years to complete. Both the interior and the exterior bear the fingerprints of George and his wife, Edith Stuyvesant Dresser. The couple's refinement, gained through international travel, educational pursuits, and cultural enrichment, is reflected in the opulence of the residence.

In affluent society of the day, it was customary to have items personalized. Edith and George embraced this tradition wholeheartedly, adding their monogram to china, crystal, silverware, serving pieces, tablecloths, napkins, toiletries, and bedding. Even the servants' livery bore the familial mark.

Above and opposite: Dining was a formal affair at Biltmore during the Gilded Age, with customized china, crystal, linens, and silver heightening luxury and ambience. Cornelia Stuyvesant Vanderbilt's monogrammed china could be used interchangeably with her father's collection.

Biltmore's official monogram is an ornate cipher with George's initials layered in elaborate script. These letters figured prominently in items used in entertaining, as well as in day-to-day life. The exterior of the château features a more stalwart *V* accented with acorns—the insignia repeated throughout the structural elements of stone and copper.

The property also houses artifacts monogrammed for George's wife, parents, and daughter. Edith's monogram was a simple *EV*, while daughter Cornelia Stuyvesant Vanderbilt's emblem was derived from George's signature cipher.

One of the most noted items on the estate to be adorned was a 1913 Stevens-Duryea C-Six. According to local legend, when the new automobile arrived, Edith found the original dark color a dismal choice. She ordered the car repainted a cheerier off-white with black pinstripes and added a feminine touch by requesting her initials be added on the rear doors. In a culture that viewed success and social rank through a monogrammed lens, the Vanderbilts reigned in a class all their own.

More than a century after its construction, Biltmore stands as a monument to American prosperity and ingenuity. With its splendid spires stretching toward the heavens, Edith and George's family home has been engraved in history.

Splendor of Christmas | 177

A perennially favorite American historic home, Mount Vernon welcomes guests year-round to explore customs practiced at the turn of the nineteenth century on the nearly 30-acre property of Martha and George Washington.

MOUNT VERNON

Despite rising to prominence as commander of the Continental Army and achieving acclaim as the father of his country, George Washington was called back throughout his life to his home at Mount Vernon, on the banks of the Potomac River in Fairfax County, Virginia. The site remains an ever-popular destination, especially during the winter months. Each year, from the day after Thanksgiving through January 6, the estate hosts Christmas at Mount Vernon. During this season of hospitality, guests can view an elaborate holiday course in the dining room and explore the usually private third floor of the Georgian mansion. Hand-cut boughs of greenery crown the doorways, and a dazzling array of opulent trees decorate the grounds.

Spectators are invited to step into the quarters during an event called Mount Vernon by Candlelight. Guides garbed as contemporaries of the first president and his wife, Martha, conduct tours of the refined interiors. Flickering embers illuminate vibrant wall colors carefully chosen through painstaking historical paint analysis, while shadows exaggerate varying architectural details. Features such as door frames, bookcases, and mouldings reflect the evolution of the home, with interior styles ranging from stark Palladianism to neoclassicism.

With his keen eye for architecture, Washington built the original two-story wooden house in 1757. Over the next forty years, the statesman renovated the dwelling, flanking it with advancing, single-story wings rendered in classic Palladian style. Sadly, he also expanded plantation operations. Even from the battlefield, and throughout two terms of his presidency, Washington personally managed the design, construction, and decoration of his beloved residence.

Antique furnishings, family heirlooms, and a few reproductions depict life in 1799. Among the treasures are a swivel chair Washington used during his time in the White House, a harpsichord he purchased for his granddaughter, and a key to the French fortress, the Bastille.

Christmas trees ornament the property with patriotic themes reflecting Washington's noble legacy as a military leader, politician, farmer, and businessman. Many ornaments and historical replicas trimming the trees are available for purchase through the gift shop.

Festivities continue at Mount Vernon with demonstrations of eighteenth-century chocolate-making techniques, period music, and dancing. In 1787, Washington paid 18 shillings for a camel to visit the property. This tradition lives on with the appearance of Aladdin the camel.

Those who experience the Christmastime delights at this historic site perhaps come to understand the president's attachment to it. "I had rather be at Mount Vernon with a friend or two about me," Washington wrote during his inaugural term, "than to be attended at the seat of government by the officers of state and the representatives of every power in Europe."

Above: Experience Yuletide splendor at the homestead of America's first president. Below right: This patriotic china plate bears the Great Seal of the United States, an official impression of the national coat of arms. With its wings displayed, a bald eagle grasps thirteen arrows in one talon and an olive branch in the other. In its beak, an unfurled scroll proclaims the Latin phrase *E Pluribus Unum*, which means "out of many, one."

Splendor of Christmas | 181

HILLS & DALES

Hills & Dales, one of the nation's foremost historic properties, crowns a gentle crest in LaGrange, Georgia. The magnificent Georgian Italian villa at the heart of the estate flows into a series of formal parterres, while woodland paths meander across lush terraces framed by magnolias and poplars. Seasonal loveliness abounds, but the splendor of Christmas offers an especially fitting tribute to the philanthropists who made this treasure available to all.

When Sarah Coleman Ferrell and her husband, Judge Blount C. Ferrell, began cultivating this acreage in 1841, the couple opened its gates to the community. During their six decades of stewardship, Ferrell Gardens became a haven of memories. Children who played in the boxwood maze matured into sweethearts courting among rose bowers. Many returned later in life, bringing their own progeny to explore the beloved terrain.

For one local boy, in particular, these enclaves represented solid ground in unsteady times. Fuller E. Callaway, who had lost his mother at age eight, often stopped by to chat. He found a maternal figure in "Miss Sarah," and even as a teenager, maintained their connection through regular Sunday afternoon walks together.

When Fuller succeeded as a textile magnate, Sarah encouraged him to continue her mission. He honored that wish in 1911, purchasing the property she had tended for sixty-two years. Fuller and his wife, Ida, christened the site Hills & Dales, built a thirty-room mansion to complement the existing parterre, and made it their residence for a quarter century. The Callaways' son Fuller Jr. inherited the home in 1936. His wife, Alice, became as deeply rooted to the landscape as the two matriarchs who had preceded her. In fact, she also managed its care for sixty-two years.

"We are so fortunate that Fuller and Alice Callaway made arrangements to preserve and share this beautiful house and garden," says Executive Director Carleton Wood. In keeping with their will, the estate opened to the public in 2004.

For the holidays, floral designer David Brown leads the staff in decorating the interiors. Cuttings gathered from the surrounding countryside highlight Alice's collections, positioned to suggest that the family has just left the room.

Tours and special events draw people to this sanctuary that once captured the imaginations of a kindly gardener and a boy destined for greatness. "Because of their vision and foresight," Wood says, "Hills & Dales will enrich the lives of future generations for years to come."

Greenery and blooms from the estate enhance seasonal vignettes. Reflecting an affinity for natural adornments are fruit in the dining room, opposite and this page, below right; topiaries in the music room, below left; and a beribboned wreath and coordinating swag affixed to a window, center left.

Above right: Plants flourish in the shelter of the greenhouse. Opposite, below right: Teacups and saucers, customized with Alice Callaway's initials, rest on a silver tray. Below left: In her French-style suite, Alice's satin wedding gown graces a chair. Personal effects on the desk include a portrait of her mother, Florence Hand, and a unique turtle clock.

Splendor of Christmas | 187

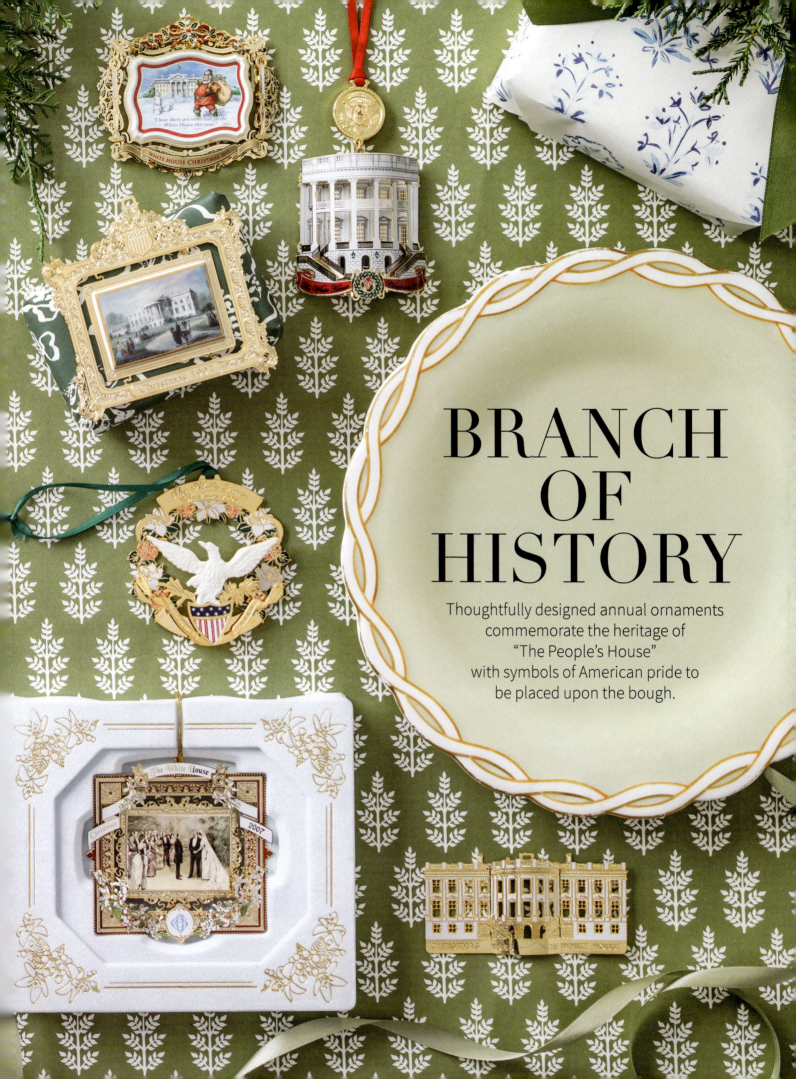

BRANCH OF HISTORY

Thoughtfully designed annual ornaments commemorate the heritage of "The People's House" with symbols of American pride to be placed upon the bough.

"CHRISTMAS IS A HOLIDAY THAT WE CELEBRATE NOT AS INDIVIDUALS NOR AS A NATION, BUT AS A HUMAN FAMILY."

—President Ronald Reagan

Like many souls who delight in the joys of travel, Robin Glawson collects precious memories of her sojourns by selecting a unique ornament to commemorate every journey. When she visits a city, whether for work or leisure, her heart finds happiness in heading home with one of these trinkets in tow—each one a token of her time spent at that enchanting destination.

A lover of American history, Robin sought to memorialize her trip to Washington, D.C., with such a treasure. While this 1996 jaunt to the nation's capital was not her first and would hardly be her last, it held something special—something that would enchant her just as much as the evergreen décor she observed throughout the city and inside the president's home itself: an official White House Christmas ornament.

Produced annually by The White House Historical Association, founded by First Lady Jacqueline Kennedy, these collectibles made their debut in 1981 with a simple, two-dimensional golden angel. Over time, Robin has gathered them all. They have been given to her by friends and family members, all aware of her growing admiration for the intricate details and fascinating stories these baubles boast.

When not displayed on a special tree in her home during the holiday season, each one is packed away in its original box, preserved alongside the pamphlet that documents the historic inspiration behind its design. Though their artistry is evident and their beauty pleasing to the eye, it is this cumulative and somehow tangible history that Robin cherishes most as she savors December's quiet moments, admiring her collection in the soft glow of Yuletide.

Designed with increasing detail, including unique imagery on either side, each gilt treasure paints a historic scene. The 2005 piece honors President James A. Garfield and features the South façade, above right, while the 2008 iteration remembers President Benjamin Harrison with a Victorian tree, below right.

Splendor of Christmas | 191

Above left: In 2017, the ornament's design included an FDR monogram, memorializing our thirty-second president's journey to restore the faith of the American people. Above right: A remarkable collectible on its own, the 2002 variety recalls the sparkling Bohemian glass of the chandeliers that hung in the East Room in 1902. Opposite: Tied with a bow, a truly unique design from 1999 bears the image of President Abraham Lincoln and opens like a book.

A COZY HEARTHSIDE REPAST

Arranged before a crackling fire, an intimate dinner for four offers respite from the bustle of the holidays. An elegant table sets a festive mood, while sumptuous seating invites guests to linger contentedly amid a banquet of delectable fare.

> "REMEMBER THIS DECEMBER,
> THAT LOVE WEIGHS MORE
> THAN GOLD!"
> —Josephine Daskam Bacon

Clockwise from left: For a refreshing starter, Roasted Beet and Citrus Salad awakens the palate with color, fragrance, and flavor. Slices of navel oranges and Ruby Red grapefruit mingle with the garnet-hued root vegetable—a vibrant foundation for leafy greens tossed in our piquant hazelnut vinaigrette. A sprinkling of pomegranate arils lends a burst of sweetness to the medley and provides a tantalizing preview of the showstopping main course. Coated in a seasoned mixture of olive oil and garlic, tender rack of lamb is first seared in the skillet and then brushed with tangy pomegranate glaze, baked to a succulent finish, and served over minty pistachio pesto.

"IT IS THE SWEET, SIMPLE THINGS OF LIFE WHICH ARE THE REAL ONES AFTER ALL."
—Laura Ingalls Wilder

Above right: Comfort food at its best, this couscous recipe combines coarsely ground grains of semolina wheat with roasted fennel and leeks. Orange zest, freshly squeezed juice, and rosemary brighten the nourishing side dish. Left: Roasted Broccolini with Crispy Sage Bread Crumbs satisfies with taste and texture. The delicate spears cook briefly in the oven—just long enough to lightly brown the brilliant bouquets at the end of each stem. The peppery stalks reach perfection when topped with a crunchy panko coating.

The culmination of this celebratory meal includes a truly indulgent pairing. Bourbon Molasses Eggnog—prepared eggnog enhanced with cream, liquor, and thick syrup—rises to the occasion in crystal stemware. Crowned with torched meringue, the beverage is presented alongside Dark Chocolate–Caramel Truffles with Sea Salt, decadent confections that won't soon be forgotten.

RECIPE INDEX

Pomegranate-Glazed Rack of Lamb
Makes 4 servings

½ cup **orange juice**
¼ cup **pomegranate juice**
2 tablespoons **honey**
2 tablespoons **balsamic vinegar**
2 tablespoons **extra-virgin olive oil**
2 cloves **garlic**, minced
½ teaspoon **kosher salt**
¼ teaspoon ground **black pepper**
1 (8-bone) **rack of lamb**, frenched*
Pistachio Pesto (recipe follows)
Garnish: **mandarin oranges, pomegranate arils, fresh herbs**

1. In a small saucepan, combine orange juice, pomegranate juice, honey, and balsamic vinegar; bring to a boil over medium-high heat. Reduce heat, and simmer until mixture is reduced to ⅓ cup.
2. Preheat oven to 450°.
3. In a small bowl, stir together olive oil, garlic, salt, and pepper. Rub mixture over lamb, and let stand for 15 minutes.
4. Heat a large oven-safe skillet over medium-high heat. Add lamb, fat-side down, and cook, without moving, until browned. Brush with pomegranate glaze. Turn lamb, and brush with glaze.
5. Place skillet in oven. Bake, fat-side up, until a thermometer inserted in thickest portion of meat registers 130°, 10 to 15 minutes, or to desired degree of doneness. Let stand for 10 minutes before cutting between bones. Serve with Pistachio Pesto, and drizzle with any remaining glaze. Garnish with oranges, pomegranate arils, and herbs, if desired.

*Ask your butcher to french the lamb, or follow our method for giving the rack a neat and elegant appearance. With bones facing up, score membrane by placing the tip of a sharp knife against the center of each bone, starting about an inch and a half from the cut end of the bone and pulling the knife slowly and firmly down the bone to its end. Using a dish towel, pull fat and membrane from between each rib slowly and firmly. It should pull away cleanly. Continue working flesh away from bones until about 2 inches are exposed. Flip the rack over, and cut away fat and membrane. Scrape away any remaining connective tissue and meat to clean the bones.

Pistachio Pesto
Makes approximately 2 cups

1 cup shelled **roasted and salted pistachios**
½ cup packed fresh **mint leaves**
½ cup packed fresh **parsley leaves**
¼ cup freshly grated **Parmesan cheese**
1 clove **garlic**
¼ teaspoon **kosher salt**
½ cup **extra-virgin olive oil**

In the work bowl of a food processor, combine pistachios, mint, parsley, Parmesan, garlic clove, and salt. Process until mixture is finely chopped. With processor running, pour olive oil through food chute in a slow, steady stream until combined. Cover and refrigerate for up to 3 days.

Roasted Beet and Citrus Salad with Hazelnut Vinaigrette
Makes 4 servings

3 large **beets**, ends trimmed
2 tablespoons **olive oil**
3 **navel oranges**, peeled and thinly sliced
2 **Ruby Red grapefruit**, peeled and thinly sliced
1 small bunch **watercress**, torn
1 small head **endive lettuce**, torn
Hazelnut Vinaigrette (recipe follows)
½ cup **pomegranate arils**

1. Preheat oven to 400°.
2. Brush beets with olive oil; wrap in heavy-duty foil, and bake directly on oven rack until beets are tender, 30 to 40 minutes. Let stand until cool enough to handle. Peel beets, and thinly slice.
3. On four individual salad plates, arrange beet slices, orange slices, and grapefruit slices.
4. In a medium bowl, toss together watercress, lettuce, and desired amount of Hazelnut Vinaigrette. Divide among serving plates. Sprinkle with pomegranate arils. Drizzle with any remaining vinaigrette, if desired.

Hazelnut Vinaigrette
Makes approximately ½ cup

3 tablespoons **Champagne vinegar**
1 tablespoon fresh **orange juice**
1 small **shallot**, minced
1 teaspoon **whole-grain mustard**
1 teaspoon **honey**
¼ teaspoon **kosher salt**
¼ teaspoon ground **black pepper**
¼ cup **extra-virgin olive oil**
½ cup finely chopped **toasted hazelnuts**

In a small bowl, whisk together vinegar, orange juice, and shallot. Let stand for 15 minutes. Whisk in mustard, honey, salt, and pepper until combined. Gradually whisk in olive oil until mixture is combined. Stir in hazelnuts. Cover and refrigerate for up to 1 week. Whisk before serving.

Roasted Fennel and Leek Couscous
Makes 4 to 6 servings

1 **fennel bulb**, thinly sliced
2 **leeks**, halved lengthwise and thinly sliced (white and pale green parts only)
3 tablespoons **olive oil**, divided
1 (10-ounce) box **plain couscous**
2 teaspoons grated **orange zest**
2 tablespoons fresh **orange juice**
1 tablespoon minced fresh **rosemary**
1 teaspoon **kosher salt**
¼ teaspoon ground **black pepper**
Garnish: fresh **dill**

1. Preheat oven to 400°. Line a baking sheet with foil.
2. On prepared pan, toss together fennel, leeks, and 2 tablespoons olive oil. Bake until fennel begins to brown and is tender, 20 to 25 minutes.
3. Meanwhile, cook couscous according to package directions; spoon into a large bowl with remaining 1 tablespoon olive oil. Add fennel mixture, orange zest, orange juice, rosemary, salt, and pepper; toss gently to combine. Serve warm or cold. Garnish with dill, if desired.

Roasted Broccolini with Crispy Sage Bread Crumbs
Makes 4 servings

3 bunches fresh **Broccolini**, trimmed
2 tablespoons **extra-virgin olive oil**
1 teaspoon **kosher salt**
2 tablespoons **butter**
2 cloves **garlic**, minced
1 cup **panko** (Japanese bread crumbs)
1 tablespoon minced fresh **sage**

1. Preheat oven to 400°. Line a baking sheet with foil.
2. On prepared baking sheet, toss together Broccolini, olive oil, and salt. Bake until Broccolini begins to brown and is tender, 10 to 12 minutes.
3. In a small skillet, melt butter over medium heat. Add garlic; cook for 30 seconds. Stir in bread crumbs, and cook, stirring constantly, until bread crumbs begin to brown, 2 to 3 minutes. Stir in sage; cook for 30 seconds.
4. Sprinkle bread crumb mixture over Broccolini, and serve immediately.

Bourbon-Molasses Eggnog with Torched Meringue
Makes 4 to 6 servings

4 cups **refrigerated eggnog**
1½ cups **heavy whipping cream**
½ cup **bourbon**
¼ cup **unsulphured molasses**
Meringue (recipe follows)
Garnish: **unsulphured molasses**

1. In a large bowl, stir together eggnog, cream, bourbon, and molasses. Cover and refrigerate for at least 4 hours.
2. To serve, pour eggnog mixture into 4 to 6 serving glasses. Top with desired amount of Meringue. Brown meringue with a culinary torch, and drizzle with molasses, if desired. Serve immediately.

Meringue
Makes approximately 3 cups

4 **egg whites**
1 cup **granulated sugar**

1. In the top of a double boiler, whisk together egg whites and sugar. Cook, whisking constantly, over simmering water until a candy thermometer registers 140°. Remove from heat.
2. Pour mixture into the work bowl of a stand mixer fitted with the whisk attachment. Beat at high speed until thick, white, and fluffy, about 10 minutes. Use immediately.

Dark Chocolate–Caramel Truffles with Sea Salt
Makes approximately 36

½ cup **granulated sugar**
3 tablespoons **water**
⅔ cup **heavy whipping cream**, warmed
1 tablespoon **light corn syrup**
1 teaspoon **sea salt**
4 (4-ounce) bars **bittersweet chocolate**, chopped and divided
Garnish: **flaked salt**

1. In a large skillet, combine sugar and 3 tablespoons water. Cook over medium-high heat, without stirring, until mixture is honey-colored. Reduce heat to low, and stir in cream, corn syrup, and sea salt, stirring until mixture is smooth. Let cool, stirring occasionally, for 15 minutes.
2. In the top of a double boiler, melt half of chocolate over simmering water. Remove from heat, and stir in caramel mixture until smooth. Cover and refrigerate until chocolate has hardened, at least 4 hours.
3. Line a rimmed baking sheet with parchment paper.
4. Using a 1-inch spring-loaded ice cream scoop, scoop chocolate mixture. Roll into 1-inch balls, and place on prepared pan. Cover and refrigerate for at least 2 hours and up to 5 days.
5. In the top of a double boiler, melt remaining half of chocolate over simmering water. Remove from heat.
6. Using 2 forks, dip truffles into melted chocolate to coat, gently tapping forks on edges of bowl to allow excess chocolate to drip off. Return to parchment-lined pan, and sprinkle with flaked salt, if desired. Repeat procedure with remaining truffles, melted chocolate, and salt. Let stand until chocolate is set, about 10 minutes. Cover and refrigerate for up to 2 weeks.

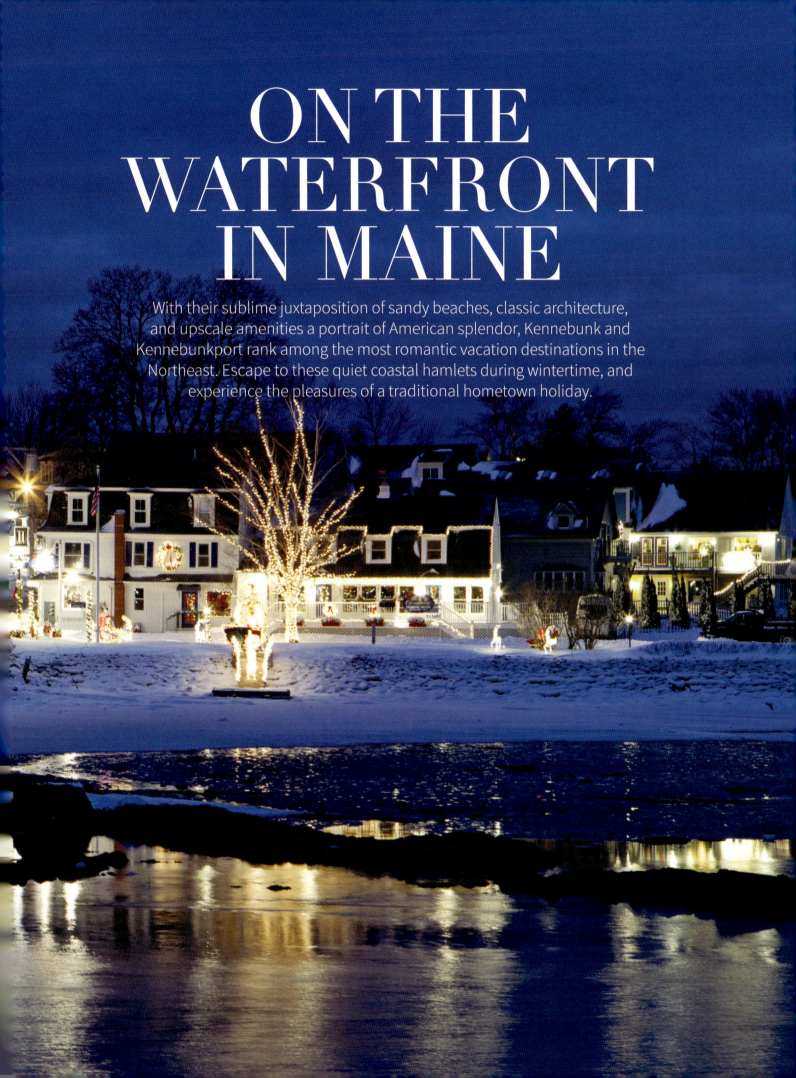

ON THE WATERFRONT IN MAINE

With their sublime juxtaposition of sandy beaches, classic architecture, and upscale amenities a portrait of American splendor, Kennebunk and Kennebunkport rank among the most romantic vacation destinations in the Northeast. Escape to these quiet coastal hamlets during wintertime, and experience the pleasures of a traditional hometown holiday.

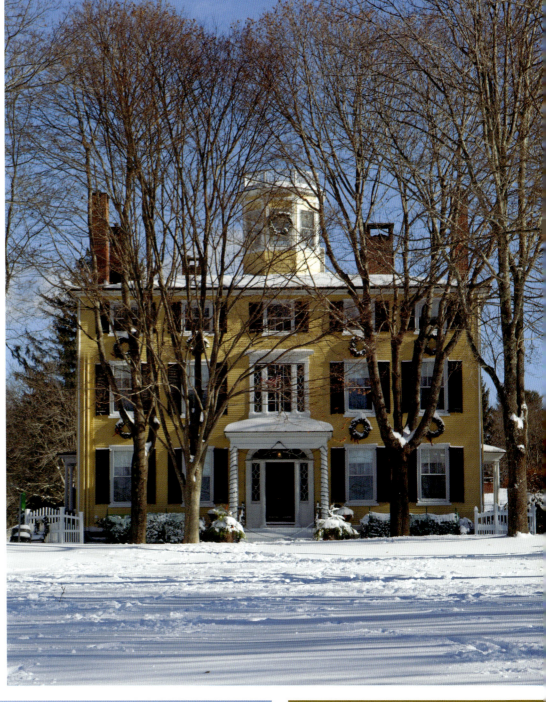

Opposite: Luxuriate in the refined environs of Nathaniel Lord Mansion, a Kennebunkport inn and spa dressed for the season in festive trimmings. This page, clockwise from above left: The stately circa 1812 to 1814 Federal-style bed-and-breakfast is located at the head of a village green in a tranquil residential area overlooking a river. Spacious quarters feature gas-burning fireplaces, four-poster beds, and prized European paintings. Along the shores of Cape Porpoise, history and scenic beauty converge. The fishing community served as Kennebunkport's original English settlement.

Take a leisurely stroll through Kennebunk to discover New England cottages brimming with creations from local artisans. With wares including textiles, photography, jewelry, and woodcrafts, this cultural haven offers homespun treasures to suit every taste.

Sojourners from as far back as the 1800s have found welcoming respite at Kennebunk Beach's White Barn Inn. Since its humble beginnings, the former summer boardinghouse has grown into an award-winning boutique hotel in the Auberge Resorts Collection. Accommodations comprise guest rooms and suites in the landmark inn, graciously appointed waterfront cottages, and a houseboat. Little extras, such as fresh flowers, plush terry cloth robes, and luxurious private-label toiletries, offer a gentle spirit of welcome. Guests savor New England cuisine in the hotel's award-winning restaurants or wine cellar.

Candlelight in the White Barn Inn Restaurant illuminates elegant linen-topped tables set with Villeroy & Boch porcelain and Schott Zwiesel crystal. In these restored stables dating from 1820, floor-to-ceiling windows frame magnificent views.

Splendor of Christmas | 209

FROM THE CONSTITUTION STATE

The postcard-pretty villages that line Route 9 epitomize the conventional notion of New England charm—a vision made even more enchanting when the calendar turns to December and the area is dressed for the season in splendor. From East Haddam and Chester to Essex and Old Lyme, these towns along the path of the Connecticut River embody the true spirit of the holidays.

Splendor of Christmas | 211

Above right: In December, the Florence Griswold Museum hosts Christmastime teas. Above left: Miss Florence's sunny chamber was once her father's sitting room. Today, the house is furnished as it was in the early twentieth century. Opposite: Elegant British furniture and accessories abound in the area's many antiques stores.

MEMORIES OF CONNECTICUT

TEXT LAURA BOGGS

Having lived in Georgia for twenty-two years, I'm an expat Yankee. I like the South, but from whence I came is in my bones. I had the outrageous good fortune of spending my formative Christmases in a Dutch Colonial house at the bottom of a long, winding drive in Connecticut.

If it sounds idyllic, it was. The grate was seldom cold in the keeping room fireplace, where I would sit as close to the flames as possible. I would read, draw, or lie with my head against our sleeping Irish setter. She, too, knew the best spot was hearthside, with a view of Mom cooking dinner in the kitchen (and the chance of a taste for both setter and me).

I miss cold New England winters. If anything, they are sincere. I remember one December snow piled so high that I had to stand on my toes to see out the first-floor windows. We had an old-fashioned wood sled with red runners and a toboggan on which the whole family plus dog could go tearing down a hill. One year, I put on my skates to shovel powder from the drive and was rewarded with an ice rink all my own.

When a blizzard came late one afternoon, I marveled at the snow comets—you could hardly call them flakes—blanketing the world in white. Dad took the train from work in Manhattan and telephoned from the local station to tell us that he and his orange Chevy were about to attempt the drive home. Later, he called to confess that a roller coaster of a back road had licked him. Not ready to admit defeat, Dad announced that he would walk home via a shortcut through the woods.

My mother, brother, and I perched at a back window, watching the trees. Mom worried, but I knew fathers are invincible, so I thought about how exquisitely hushed the woods must sound—the quietest quiet of all is outdoors in snow. Hours later, the dog barked wildly as the abominable snowman appeared, laughing about his adventure.

On Christmas mornings, I would find pristine ice skates under the tree. There were plenty of opportunities to make use of skates on frozen ponds all over town. But the desire of my heart was for Dad to cut the blades off mine so I could wear the lace-up boots every day, evoking *Little House on the Prairie*. (Never mind that my skates were white, not frontier black.) Mom quashed that idea.

I wanted to be various things at Yuletide—Laura Ingalls, of course, which wasn't hard to imagine with my long nut-brown hair pulled into tight braids.

But my first Christmas love—in fact, my first love, period—was Santa Claus, and by the time I could hold a Crayola, I drew the jolly old elf on pieces of scrap paper and in the margins of my mother's cookbook, flipped open to the holiday cookie pages. When I was very small, I informed fellow preschoolers that I intended to marry Saint Nick. You can't do that, someone said. Someone was always Pointing Things Out.

One Pointer-Outer was my slightly older neighbor, Tina G., who felt it was her duty to apprise me of Facts. "Think about it," she said. "How could a fat man squeeze down a chimney flue? And what of the time constraint of delivering gifts to the entire planet in one night? And flying reindeer?" I had an inimitably logical answer for all of it. Tina G. got my attention, though: "It's your parents, Silly."

And so I ran inside and asked my mother. Mom toed the line, but during the next few weeks, I asked and asked until a tragic Christmas Eve when, as Mom was at the stove stirring oyster stew, I asked her once more. "Well," she said absentmindedly as she tended the pot, "what do you think?"

What! Adults never asked children what they thought—unless they were trying to gently coax them toward the correct answer, the proper view of things. And so the scales fell from my eyes.

"You've been lying to me my entire life!" I shouted. I cried and keened for the next few hours as Mom sat with inconsolable me, and visiting relatives ate supper without us. Oh, the drama.

I don't hold it against my parents—telling me this fantastic tale. In fact, I'm glad they did. What would a kid in Connecticut, her moony face pressed against the glass to stare at the evening's indigo snow, do without a fairy story or two to believe in?

WRAPPED IN COLONIAL STYLE

Tallwood is swathed in an elegance reminiscent of early settlers' celebrations, with an added touch of glamour.

Before the calendar resets, former *Victoria* Artist-in-Residence Jenny Bohannon marks the season with Yuletide displays steeped in tradition. A flock of Leicester Longwool sheep grazes in the field, bleating a welcome as doors open to reveal a dining table laden with fresh fruit, pine cones, seashells, and sprigs of greenery, emulating the foraging of Virginia colonists.

Centering the history-inspired theme is reproduction china that echoes natural elements with colorful finds from orchard and vineyard. Displayed in the museum collections of Colonial Williamsburg, a dinner service designed in 1770 for the brother of King George III inspired Mottahedeh's popular Duke of Gloucester pattern.

Jenny's distinctive holiday trimmings, which highlight hues beyond the customary red and green, arise from years of study—a dedication that informs her design choices throughout the year. "We have to train our eyes," she explains, encouraging homeowners to look "through the lens of those who have very good taste." The content creator often remarks on the role of past tastemakers in helping cultivate her style. As with painting or playing an instrument, she points out that the art of making a home comes with practice, time, and observation.

At Yuletide, thrifted glassware, flatware, and silver pieces placed atop Julia Amory linens threaded with moss-colored vines ready the dining room for breakfast, complete with homemade baked goods delivered by a friend. Yet as Jenny's family wakes on Christmas morning, rubbing sleepy eyes to peer under the festive bauble-draped tree, her ultimate role in the home finds fulfillment in the joy on her children's faces. "My heart," she says, "is for women to feel that homemaking is such a gift to a family."

Splendor of Christmas | 217

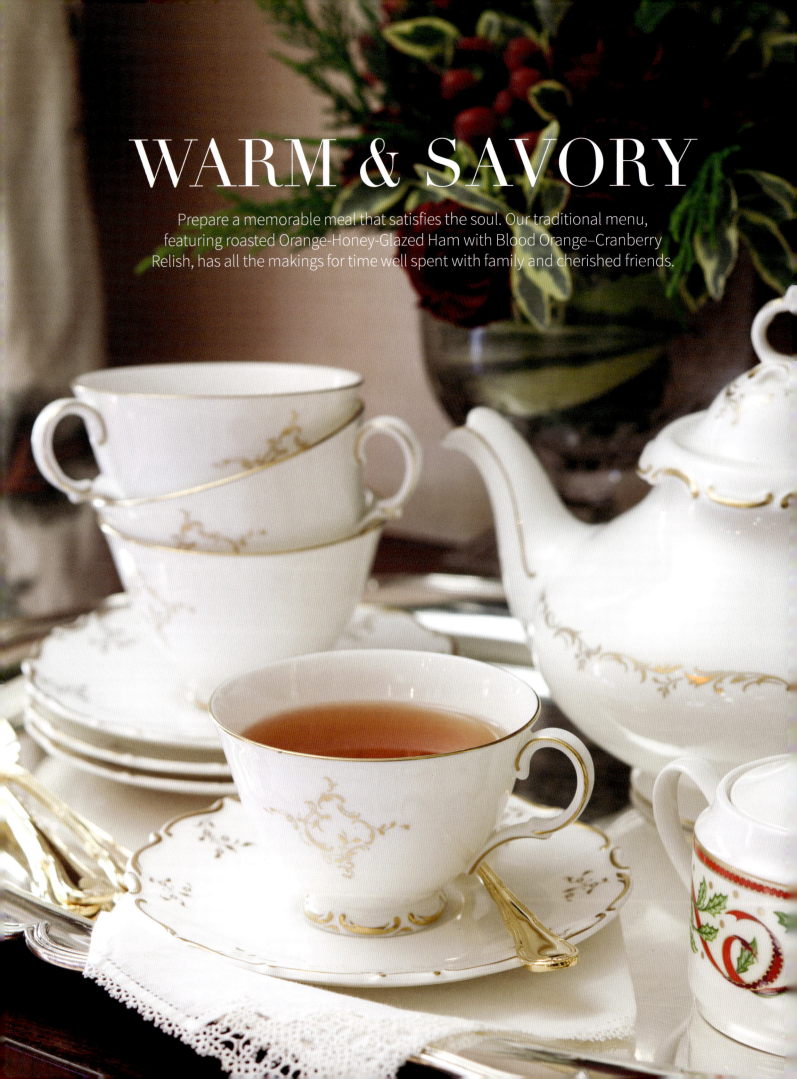

WARM & SAVORY

Prepare a memorable meal that satisfies the soul. Our traditional menu, featuring roasted Orange-Honey-Glazed Ham with Blood Orange–Cranberry Relish, has all the makings for time well spent with family and cherished friends.

A sit-down dinner served with gracious hospitality is the best way to treat loved ones to an array of home-cooked favorites. White china dinnerware with gold embellishments and understated Christmas motifs provides a flattering backdrop for eye-catching accents of red roses, crimson berries, and fresh greenery. Clear crystal stemware, gleaming silver flatware, and flickering white tapers shimmer with holiday elegance.

Splendor of Christmas

Opposite: Whet your appetite with a steaming bowl of Roasted Cauliflower and Parsnip Soup—the ideal starter on a chilly December day. A smooth concoction created with a purée of cauliflower, parsnips, half-and-half, chicken broth, yellow onion, and garlic, our recipe is seasoned with black and white pepper and ground nutmeg. A topping of crispy pancetta and oregano brings robust flavor and a pleasing aroma to this nourishing wintertime specialty.

This page, above left: A Christmas gathering wouldn't be complete without the delectable scent of baking bread wafting from the oven. Melt-in-your-mouth Clover Leaf Rolls are designed to pull apart with ease or to wedge with pats of creamy butter. These crowd-pleasing accompaniments can be served alongside soup or with the entire meal.

Right: A classic side dish gets a vibrant seasonal twist with our Sweet Potato Gratin. Layers of sliced sweet potatoes drizzled with browned butter and garlic-and-herb-infused chicken broth bake to a toasty golden brown in a springform pan. Allow the finished gratin to cool and set before inverting onto a serving platter. For an added burst of color and taste, sprinkle with chopped thyme.

Above: A delightfully savory alternative to a traditional holiday turkey, a Christmas ham roasted to juicy perfection always meets with resounding approval. We paired Orange-Honey-Glazed Ham with Blood Orange–Cranberry Relish mixed with golden raisins, Granny Smith apples, pomegranate arils, and fennel seeds. This brightly flavored fusion beautifully balances the sweet-and-salty taste combination of ham brushed with honey glaze.

Left: Round out the colorful presentation with deliciously tender Green Bean and Onion Sauté. This garden-fresh medley features French green beans, purple pearl onions, celery, and shallots cooked in butter until lightly browned. For a fragrant and nutty finish, mix in thinly shaved fennel and toasted sliced almonds before serving.

Opposite: Punctuate this gathering with our magnificent Rum Cake with Orange Liqueur Glaze. Made with spiced rum and crowned with sugared cranberries, this celebratory dessert will entice guests to linger at the table a bit longer for coffee, conversation, and perhaps a second helping.

RECIPE INDEX

Roasted Cauliflower and Parsnip Soup
Makes 6 to 8 servings (8½ cups)

1 head **cauliflower**, chopped and stem removed
6 **parsnips**, peeled and chopped
1 (4-ounce) package **deli-sliced pancetta**
1 cup chopped **yellow onion**
1 clove **garlic**, peeled and chopped
3 cups **chicken broth**
2 cups **water**
½ teaspoon **kosher salt**
½ teaspoon ground **white pepper**
¼ teaspoon ground **black pepper**
¼ teaspoon ground **nutmeg**
2 cups **half-and-half**
Garnish: fresh **oregano**

1. Preheat oven to 400°. Line a baking sheet with foil; spray with cooking spray.
2. Arrange cauliflower and parsnips on prepared pan. Roast until browned, 20 to 25 minutes. Remove from oven and let cool completely.
3. In a stockpot, cook pancetta until crisp. Remove pancetta from pot, and set aside, reserving grease.
4. To same pot, add onion and garlic. Cook over medium heat, stirring often, until slightly browned and tender, about 5 minutes. Add broth, 2 cups water, prepared cauliflower and parsnips, salt, white pepper, black pepper, and nutmeg; bring to a boil. Reduce heat and simmer for about 10 minutes. Remove from heat and let cool for 30 minutes.
5. In a blender, purée mixture in batches until smooth. Add half-and-half, stir to combine, and return mixture to pot. Cook over medium-low heat, stirring often, until heated thoroughly. Top with prepared pancetta, and garnish with oregano, if desired. Serve warm.

Clover Leaf Rolls
Makes 18

3 tablespoons plus 2 teaspoons firmly packed **light brown sugar**, divided
1 cup warm **milk** (110° to 115°)
1 (¼-ounce) package **active dry yeast**
3½ cups **bread flour**, divided
1 teaspoon **salt**
1 large **egg**
3 tablespoons **butter**, melted and cooled

1. Spray a large bowl with cooking spray.
2. In a separate large bowl, combine 1 teaspoon brown sugar, milk, and yeast. Let mixture sit until foamy, about 5 minutes. Add 1 cup flour; beat with a mixer at medium-low speed until combined, about 2 minutes. Add salt, egg, and butter, and beat until combined. Add remaining 2 tablespoons plus 2 teaspoons brown sugar and remaining 2½ cups flour, and beat just until combined. Place dough in prepared bowl; spray top of dough with cooking spray. Cover loosely with plastic wrap, and refrigerate for at least 8 hours or overnight. (Dough will rise and double in size.)
3. Spray 1 (12-cup) muffin pan and 1 (6-cup) muffin pan with cooking spray.
4. Turn out dough and punch down. Divide into 54 even pieces. Gently shape each piece into a 1-inch ball, coating hands with cooking spray as needed. Place 3 balls in each muffin cup. Spray rolls with cooking spray, cover loosely with plastic wrap, and let rise in a warm, draft-free place (80°) until doubled in size, about 60 minutes.
5. Preheat oven to 375°.
6. Bake until lightly browned, about 15 minutes. Remove from oven and let cool in pans for 5 minutes. Remove from pans and brush with additional melted butter, if desired. Serve warm.

Sweet Potato Gratin
Makes 6 to 8 servings

1½ cups **chicken broth**
2 **garlic cloves**, peeled and halved
2 sprigs fresh **rosemary**
2 sprigs fresh **thyme**
1 tablespoon **black peppercorns**
5 large **sweet potatoes**, scrubbed and sliced ⅛ inch thick
½ cup **browned butter***, melted
Garnish: fresh **thyme**

1. In a small saucepan, combine broth, garlic, rosemary, thyme, and peppercorns. Bring to a boil over high heat. Reduce heat and simmer until reduced by half (¾ cup), about 10 minutes. Remove from heat and strain through a fine-mesh sieve, discarding solids.
2. Preheat oven to 350°. Spray a 9-inch springform pan with cooking spray. Line bottom of pan with a round of parchment paper, and spray again. Place pan on a piece of foil, and wrap to enclose base and sides of pan. Place springform pan on a rimmed baking sheet.
3. Place a layer of potatoes in prepared pan, overlapping slices and covering bottom of pan. Drizzle with broth mixture and browned butter. Repeat layers until all potatoes, broth, and butter are used. Cover with foil.
4. Bake for 45 minutes to 1 hour. Remove foil, and bake until top layer of potatoes is slightly browned, 15 to 20 minutes more. Remove from oven and let cool, about 15 minutes.
5. Carefully remove foil from pan. Release pan (be careful, as excess liquid may drain from pan when released), and invert onto a cutting board. Invert again onto a serving platter. Garnish with thyme, if desired. Serve warm.

*In a medium saucepan, melt butter over medium heat. Cook until butter turns a medium-brown color and has a nutty aroma, about 10 minutes. Remove from heat, and let cool to room temperature. Use immediately, or cover and refrigerate for up to 1 week.

Orange-Honey-Glazed Ham
Makes approximately 8 servings

1 cup **water**
1 (12-pound) bone-in **cured ham**
20 whole **cloves**
Honey Glaze (recipe follows)
Blood Orange–Cranberry Relish (recipe follows)
Garnish: fresh **sage**

1. Preheat oven to 325°. Pour 1 cup water into a large roasting pan.
2. Using a sharp knife, score fat on ham in a crosshatch pattern; stud ham with cloves. Place ham, flat side down, in prepared roasting pan; cover loosely with foil.

3. Bake, basting every hour with pan juices, until a meat thermometer inserted in thickest part of ham registers 135°, about 4 hours. Remove from oven, and brush with Honey Glaze. Let ham sit for 15 minutes, and brush with glaze again. Serve with any remaining glaze and Blood Orange–Cranberry Relish. Garnish with sage, if desired.

Honey Glaze
Makes 1½ cups

½ cup firmly packed **light brown sugar**
½ cup **honey**
¼ cup **orange juice**
¼ cup **Dijon mustard**

In a small saucepan, whisk together brown sugar, honey, orange juice, and mustard. Bring mixture to a boil over medium-high heat. Reduce heat and simmer, whisking occasionally, until sugar is dissolved, 3 to 4 minutes. Remove from heat, and let cool completely.

Blood Orange–Cranberry Relish
Makes approximately 3 cups

4 **blood oranges**
1 (10-ounce) bag **frozen cranberries**
½ cup firmly packed **light brown sugar**
1½ cups **golden raisins**
1½ cups chopped **Granny Smith apple**
1 cup **pomegranate arils**
2 tablespoons **fennel seed**
Garnish: fresh **parsley**

1. Using a Y-shaped vegetable peeler, peel skin from oranges in long, thick strips. Using a kitchen knife, coarsely chop orange peel. Into a measuring cup, squeeze 1 cup juice from oranges.
2. In a small saucepan, combine orange peel, orange juice, cranberries, and brown sugar. Bring to a boil over high heat. Reduce heat to medium-high, and cook, stirring often, until thickened, about 10 minutes. Remove from heat, and let cool completely.
3. Add raisins, apple, pomegranate arils, and fennel seed, stirring to combine. Refrigerate for at least 4 hours before serving. Garnish with parsley, if desired.

Green Bean and Onion Sauté
Makes 6 to 8 servings

¼ cup **butter**, divided
2 pounds **French green beans**, trimmed
1 (10-ounce) bag **purple pearl onions**, blanched and peeled
3 stalks **celery**, chopped
3 **shallots**, quartered
1 teaspoon **kosher salt**
1 teaspoon ground **black pepper**
½ **fennel bulb**, shaved thin
½ cup toasted sliced **almonds**

1. In a large nonstick pan, melt 2 tablespoons butter over medium-high heat. Add beans, in batches, cooking until lightly browned. Remove from pan and set aside.
2. Melt remaining 2 tablespoons butter over medium-high heat. Add pearl onions, celery, and shallots, and cook until lightly browned. Add beans back to pan, stirring to combine; season with salt and pepper, and cook over medium heat until heated thoroughly. Remove from heat. Stir in fennel and almonds. Serve warm.

Rum Cake with Orange Liqueur Glaze
Makes 1 (10-cup) Bundt cake

1¾ cups **unsalted butter**, softened
2 cups firmly packed **light brown sugar**
4 large **eggs**
2 **egg yolks**
1 tablespoon **vanilla extract**
2 teaspoons **rum extract**
3½ cups **all-purpose flour**
2½ teaspoons **baking powder**
1 teaspoon **baking soda**
1 teaspoon **salt**
1½ cups **heavy whipping cream**
¾ cup **spiced rum**
Orange Liqueur Glaze (recipe follows)
Garnish: **sugared cranberries**, **sugared rosemary**

1. Preheat oven to 350°. Spray a 10-cup Bundt pan* with baking spray with flour.
2. In a large bowl, beat butter and brown sugar with a mixer at medium-high speed until fluffy, about 3 minutes.
3. Add eggs, one at a time, beating well after each addition, scraping down sides of bowl, as needed. Add egg yolks, one at a time, beating well after each addition. Add vanilla extract and rum extract, beating to combine.
4. In a medium bowl, whisk together flour, baking powder, baking soda, and salt.
5. To a 4-cup measuring cup, add cream and rum, whisking to combine.
6. Add flour mixture to butter mixture in thirds, alternating with cream mixture, beginning and ending with flour mixture. Pour batter into prepared pan.
7. Bake until a wooden pick inserted near center comes out clean, 60 to 75 minutes. Remove from oven, and let cool in pan on a wire rack for 10 minutes. Invert pan onto wire rack, and let cool completely.
8. Pour Orange Liqueur Glaze over cake, and garnish with sugared cranberries and sugared rosemary, if desired.

*We used a Nordic Ware cast-aluminum Kugelhopf 10-cup Bundt Pan.

Orange Liqueur Glaze
Makes approximately 1½ cups

1½ cups **confectioners' sugar**
2 tablespoons **orange juice**
2 tablespoons **orange liqueur**

In a small bowl, whisk together confectioners' sugar, orange juice, and orange liqueur until smooth. Use immediately or store in an airtight container at room temperature for up to 5 days.

Splendor of Christmas

CREDITS & RESOURCES

Splendor of Christmas: English, French, and American Holiday Style

Editor: Melissa Lester
Creative Director, Lifestyle: Melissa Sturdivant Smith
Senior Features Editors: Lydia McMullen, Audra Shalles, Leslie Bennett Smith
Administrative Senior Art Director: Tracy Wood-Franklin
Senior Copy Editor, Lifestyle: Rhonda Lee Lother
Senior Digital Imaging Specialist: Delisa McDaniel

CONTRIBUTING WRITERS

KASSIDY ABERNATHY: pages 52–55
LAURA BOGGS: page 215
KATIE BRANDON: pages 72–79
KAREN CALLAWAY: pages 12–43, 106–115, and 138–143
JEANNE DE LATHOUDER: pages 218–223
BRITTANY FLOWERS: pages 44–49 and 84–93
MELISSA LESTER: pages 9, 11, 83, 116–125, 143, 149, 153, 173–187
LYDIA MCMULLEN: pages 94–105, 128–137, and 216
NANCY A. RUHLING: pages 154–163
AUDRA SHALLES: pages 56–65
LESLIE BENNETT SMITH: pages 66–71 and 188–193
WILMA TJALSMA-SMITS: pages 128–137

CONTRIBUTING PHOTOGRAPHERS

JENNY BOHANNON: pages 216–217
LEWIS BUSH, COURTESY ©CHARLES DICKENS MUSEUM: pages 52–55
CARYN B. DAVIS: pages 210–214
LOUIS GAILLARD: pages 138–143
KATE HEADLEY: pages 178–181
JANE HOPE: pages 10, 12–21, and 34–43
MAC JAMIESON: pages 75, 78, 144–145, 148–149, and 177
GEORGIANNA LANE: pages 6, 22–33, and 94–105
PIERRE NICOU: pages 84–93 and 106–115
KATE SEARS: pages 152, 154–163 and 202–209
MARCY BLACK SIMPSON: pages 1, 4–5, 44–49, 72–74, 81, 164–175, 182–187, and 218–223
KELLY SLIWA: pages 146–148
CAROLINE SMITH: page 79
STEPHANIE WELBOURNE STEELE: cover and pages 8, 116–125, 188–199, and 201
JOYCE VLOET: pages 128–137

CONTRIBUTING STYLISTS

COREY AMARO: pages 106–115
JENNY BOHANNON: pages 216–217
SIDNEY BRAGIEL: pages 116–125
MARIE-PAULE FAURE: pages 84–93 and 138–143
JANE HOPE: pages 34–43
LINDSAY KEITH KESSLER: pages 72–79
JORDAN MARXER MILLNER: pages 210–213
YUKIE MCLEAN: pages 144–149
MELISSA STURDIVANT SMITH: pages 8, 72–74, 79, 81, 188–193, 194–199, and 201
KATHLEEN COOK VARNER: pages 44–49 and 202–209

CONTRIBUTING RECIPE DEVELOPERS AND FOOD STYLISTS

KATHLEEN KANEN: pages 116–127
LEAH PEREZ: pages 116–127
REBECCA TREADWELL SPRADLING: pages 194–201
LOREN WOOD: pages 44–51, 72–81, 144–151, and 218–225

WHERE TO SHOP & BUY

Below is a listing of properties, products, and companies featured in this book. Items not listed are privately owned and are not for sale. Styles and availability may vary.

Page 8: Private collection provided by Lance Britt, The Brittany House Antiques at Oak Hill, 5931 AL-21, Oak Hill, AL, @thebrittanyhouseantiques on Instagram.

Pages 12–21: Castle Howard Estate, York, YO60 7DA, England, castlehoward.co.uk.

Pages 22–33: Fortnum & Mason, 181 Piccadilly, St. James's, London WIA IER, UK, fortnumandmason.com. Cartier, 175–177 New Bond Street, Mayfair, London W1S 4RN, UK, cartier.co.uk. Piccadilly Arcade, St. James's, London SW1Y 6NH, UK, piccadilly-arcade.com. The Lanesborough, Hyde Park Corner, London SW1X 7TA, UK, oetkercollection.com/hotels/the-lanesborough/. The Ivy, 1–5 West Street, London WC2H 9NQ, UK, ivycollection.com/restaruants/the-ivy-west-street/. Lola's Cupcakes, 14–18 Neal Street, Covent Garden, WC2H 9LY, London UK, lolascupcakes.co.uk. Harrods, 87–135 Brompton Road, Knightsbridge, London SW1X 7XL, UK, harrods.com. Natural History Museum, Cromwell Road, Kensington, London SW7 5BD, UK, nhm.ac.uk. The Ritz London, 150 Piccadilly, St. James's, London W1J 9BR, UK, theritzlondon.com. Liberty London, Regent Street, Carnaby, London W1B 5AH, UK, libertylondon.com. Corinthia Hotel London, Whitehall Place, Westminster, London SW1A 2BD, UK, corinthia.com. Leadenhall Market, Gracechurch Street, London EC3V 1LT, UK, cityoflondon.gov.uk. Bea's of Bloomsbury, 44 Theobalds Road, London WC1X 8NW, beasofbloomsbury.com. Burlington Arcade, 51 Piccadilly, Mayfair, LondonW1J 0QJ, UK, burlingtonarcade.com. Rosewood London, 252 High Holborn, London WC1V 7EN, UK, rosewoodhotels.com. La Fromagerie, 2–4 Moxon Street, Marylebone, London W1U 4EW, UK, lafromagerie.co.uk.

Pages 44–49: Antique floral painting, brass urn, brass candelabras, pipe, brass vase, cane, white teapot, dessert plate; from Tricia's Treasures, triciastreasures.us. Antique punch bowl and cups, and ironstone tureen; from Attic Antiques, atticantiquesal.com. Lenox: Holiday Tartan 5-piece place setting, Holiday Tartan Fruit/Dessert bowl, Holiday Tartan 13" Oval Serving Platter; Towle Old Colonial 5-piece place setting; Fostoria Jamestown Brown Water Goblet; from Replacements, Ltd., replacements.com.

Pages 52–55: Special thanks to the Charles Dickens Museum for use of photography. Charles Dickens Museum, 48–49 Doughty Street, London, WC1N 2LX, England, dickensmuseum.com.

Pages 56–65: Special thanks to Chatsworth House Trust for use of photography. Chatsworth House, Bakewell, Derbyshire DE45 1PP, UK, chatsworth.org.

Pages 66–71: Special thanks to Highclere Castle for use of photography. Highclere Castle, Highclere Park, Newbury RG20 9RN, UK, highclerecastle.co.uk. *Christmas at Highclere: Recipes and Traditions from The Real Downton Abbey* by The Countess of Carnarvon, available at victoriamag.com/shop.

Pages 72–79: All flowers and greenery from Hall's Birmingham Wholesale Florist; hallsbirmingham.com.

Pages 94–105: À La Mère de la Famille, 35 Rue du Faubourg Montmartre, Paris, France, lameredefamille.com. Angelina, 226 Rue de Rivoli, Paris, France, angelina-paris.fr. Eiffel Tower, Avenue Gustave Eiffel, Paris, France, toureiffel.paris/fr. Galeries Lafayette Champs-Élysées, 60 Avenue des Champs-Élysées, Paris, France, galerieslafayette.com. Galerie Vivienne, 4 Rue des Petits-Champs, Paris, France, galerie-vivienne.com. Ladurée Paris Champs Elysées, 75 Avenue des Champs Elysées, Paris, France, laduree.fr. Printemps Haussmann, 64 Boulevard Haussmann, Paris, France, printemps.com. Salon Proust, 15 Place Vendôme, Paris, France, ritzparis.com/hotel/paris/bars-restaurants/salon-proust.

Pages 106–115: Corey Amaro, stylist and lifestyle blogger, frenchlavie.com.

Pages 116–125: Mottahedeh: Duke of Gloucester Cup & Saucer, Duke of Gloucester Large Ginger Jar & Lid, Duke of Gloucester Dessert Plate, Gabriel Currant Dinner Plate; mottahedeh.com. Kim Seybert: Pave Placemat; from CB Lifestyle, shopcblifestyle.com. Haviland: 10" Oval Serving Platter in Schleiger 133; from Replacements, Ltd., replacements.com. Herend: Ribbon Tray; herendusa.com.

Pages 128–137: Special thanks to Peet! and Coco Features. Special thanks to homeowners Marlies and Ralph; book a stay on their property at lapetiteporcherie.nl.

Pages 138–143: Caron Paris, parfumscaron.com/en.

Pages 144–149: Floral arrangements from Dorothy McDaniel's Flower Market, dorothymcdaniel.com. Champagne glasses; from Bromberg's, brombergs.com.

Pages 154–163: Seasons of Williamsburg, 1308 Jamestown Road, Williamsburg, VA, shopatseasons.com.

Pages 164–171: Colonial Williamsburg: Openwork Creamware, Duke of Gloucester dinnerware, Crystal Airtwist stemware, Shell sterling flatware, Winter's Garland mug, Winter's Garland dessert plates; shop.colonialwilliamsburg.com.

Pages 172–187: Special thanks to Biltmore House for use of photography. Biltmore, 1 Lodge Street, Asheville, NC, biltmore.com. Mount Vernon, 3200 Mount Vernon Memorial Highway, Mount Vernon, VA, mountvernon.org. Hills & Dales Estate, 1916 Hills and Dales Drive, LaGrange, GA, hillsanddales.org.

Pages 188–193: Special thanks to collection owner Robin Glawson. The White House Historical Association: Full White House Christmas Ornament Collection, Window with Tree Ornament; shop.whitehousehistory.org.

Pages 194–199: Lenox: Dinner Plate in Rococo Leaf, Salad Plate in Rococo Leaf, Bread & Butter Plate in Rococo Leaf; from Replacements, Ltd., replacements.com.

Pages 202–209: Lark Hotels Kennebunkport Captains Collection: Nathaniel Lord Mansion, 6 Pleasant Street, Kennebunkport, ME, larkhotels.com/hotels/kennebunkport-captains-collection. The White Barn Inn, 37 Beach Avenue, Kennebunk, ME, aubergeresorts.com/whitebarninn.

Pages 210–213: The Griswold Inn, 36 Main Street, Essex, CT, griswoldinn.com. Florence Griswold Museum, 96 Lyme Street, Old Lyme, CT, florencegriswoldmuseum.org. Leif Nilsson Spring Street Studio and Gallery, 1 Spring Street, Chester, CT, nilssonstudio.com.

Pages 216–217: Special thanks to Jenny Bohannon of Tallwood, tallwoodcountryhouse.com and @tallwoodcountryhouse on Instagram.

Pages 218–223: Royal Doulton: Monteigne Footed Cup & Saucer, Monteigne Teapot & Lid; Wedgwood: Ascot Dinner Plate; from Replacements, Ltd., replacements.com. Pickard: Winter Festival White Sugar Bowl & Cover, Winter Festival White 5-piece Place Setting; pickardchina.com. Herend Golden Edge Cream Soup Cup, Ribbon Tray, Chop Plate with Handles; herendusa.com. Reed & Barton: silverplate tray, Hammered Antique Carving Set; from Bromberg's, brombergs.com.

RECIPE INDEX

Ambrosia Scones 80
Blood Orange–Cranberry Relish 225
Bourbon-Molasses Eggnog with Torched Meringue 201
Bûche de Noël 126
Buttermilk–Grand Marnier Panna Cotta 151
Chicken Salad Sandwiches with Cranberry-Apricot Chutney 80
Chocolate Buttercream 127
Chocolate, Cherry, and Hazelnut Terrine 150
Chocolate-Toffee Truffles 151
Cinnamon-Caramel Sauce 51
Clover Leaf Rolls 224
Cranberry-Apricot Chutney 81
Dark Chocolate–Caramel Truffles with Sea Salt 201
Figgy Pudding 51
Gratin Dauphinois 126
Green Bean and Onion Sauté 225
Haricots Verts Amandine 126
Hazelnut Vinaigrette 200
Honey Glaze 225
Meringue 201
Meringue Mushrooms 127
Mini Pear Galettes 150
Orange-Honey-Glazed Ham 224
Orange Liqueur Glaze 225
Orange-Scented Pear Turnovers 80
Oyster Soup 50
Pistachio Pesto 200
Pistachio Shortbread 151
Pomegranate-Glazed Rack of Lamb 200
Poulet au Vinaigre 125
Prosciutto, Tomato, and Ricotta Tarts 80
Pumpkin Chai Pots de Crème 150
Roasted Beet and Citrus Salad with Hazelnut Vinaigrette 200
Roasted Broccolini with Crispy Sage Bread Crumbs 201
Roasted Cauliflower and Parsnip Soup 224
Roasted Christmas Goose 50
Roasted Fennel and Leek Couscous 200
Roasted Root Vegetables 51
Rum Cake with Orange Liqueur Glaze 225
Sage and Browned Butter Mashed Potatoes 51
Smoked Salmon Sesame Crisps 125
Smoking Bishop 50
Sugared Cranberries with Simple Syrup 127
Sweet Potato Gratin 224
Tartes de Linz 150
Vanilla Bean Buttercream 127
Yorkshire Puddings 50